A GLIMPSE
OF
GLORY

SEEING GOD IN THE MIDST OF IT ALL

MANAGING EDITOR

Timeko Whitaker

a.i.c.

Authentic Identity Coaching

PUBLISHED BY
Authentic Identity Coaching, LLC
P.O. Box 36131
Indianapolis, IN 46236

www.authenticinstitute.com
authenticidentity@gmail.com
(317) 710-9533

Please contact
Authentic Identity Coaching
for quantity discounts

©2017 Timeko Whitaker
ISBN: 978-0-9863401-2-3
Library of Congress Number: 2017901146
Printed in the United States of America

Editing & Book Layout by ASAP
Writing Services
Cover Design and Photography by
Xzibitz Portraits & Design

TABLE OF CONTENTS

About the Managing Editor

Introduction

Authentic Identity Services & Resources

ABOUT THE MANAGING EDITOR

Timeko L. Whitaker, Founder CEO of Authentic Identity Coaching, LLC, is the wife of Eric Whitaker and the mother of Daelin and Eyuana Whitaker. She is a gifted Life Coach and International Speaker who challenges all to live an authentic life on purpose. Timeko holds a Bachelor's Degree in Human Resource Management and a Master's Degree in Theology.

Timeko is a certified Human Behavior Consultant (specializing in DISC) and a certified Life Coach. Her coaching sessions are life changing and impact attendees of all demographical backgrounds while her "5D Authentically Me™" empowerment seminars continue to empower clients both locally and internationally.

Timeko is a certified John Maxwell Team Member, Speaker, Trainer and Coach equipped to develop and train worldwide leaders. Timeko is a publishing manager of *Hidden Identity-Untold Stories of Pastor's Wives* and a contributing author of *The Power of Mentorship* with Zig Ziglar, Brian Tracy and other amazing authors. Timeko is also the Managing Editor/Publisher of *A Piece of Me – My Journey of Authenticity*.

Timeko enjoys spending time as a part-time host on TBN's WCLJ-TV's "Joy In Our Town" where she interviews community leaders, businesses, and organizations that make a difference in our society.

In 2015 Timeko and her husband Eric launched Authentic Identity Institute where they train and certify 5D Identity Coaches and Human Behavior Consultants. Timeko's goal is to help everyone she encounters embrace their authenticity and significance. Through speaking, training and coaching she motivates all to reach higher heights, embrace values and achieve their dreams.

With over twenty years of military service, culminating in her retirement in 2008, coupled with ten years of pastoral service; Timeko has committed her life to serving God through serving others and has dedicated her business to helping all discover the power of authenticity. To date, Authentic Identity Institute has coached over 50 authors to share their story in published books.

Authentic Identity Coaching, LLC
PO Box 36131, Indianapolis, IN 46236
317-710-9533
AuthenticIdentity@gmail.com
www.AuthenticInstitute.com
www.JohnMaxwellGroup.com/TimekoWhitaker

Introduction

John, 11:40, *Jesus said to her, "Did I not say to you that if you believe, you will see the glory of God?*

As a Certified Christian Life Coach, there's nothing more fulfilling than witnessing the authentic journey of one who believes enough to move past every block and barrier to pursue and embrace the call upon their lives. Daily, I encounter amazing people with untold stories that if fully revealed would send shockwaves through the very heart of any reader, yet they continue their relentless walk of faith.

Each of these authors have partnered with Authentic Identity Coaching and allowed us to play a small part in the BIG that God is doing in their lives. These strong, bold, and courageous men and women of God have all embraced the idea that they are to be good stewards over not only their time, talents, and treasures but also over their testimonies. They've come to a realization that the significance of their past can aid in bringing others out of a place of pain and into a place of permission... Permission to move forward, permission to forgive, permission to allow God's glory to be revealed through their story.

Our hope is that each chapter and testimony

will ignite something deep on the inside of you that will give you strength and courage to maneuver past obstacles and to advance in life. We pray the words will emanate from the pages to bring life to every dead situation you may be facing. We pray to bring hope and reassurance that your life has only just begun and as you move forward in faith, you'll embrace the truth that the best is yet to come. Journey with us as we give God all the glory.

Timeko Whitaker
Managing Editor

A GLIMPSE
OF GLORY

Be exalted above the heavens, O God;
Let Your glory be above all the earth.
Psalm 57:5 NIV

Tracy Pruitt

Tracy Pruitt is a servant-leader, teacher, licensed counselor, conference speaker, relationship builder, and a first time author.

A native of Indianapolis, IN., Tracy credits her academic discipline to the Indianapolis Public School System and is a proud graduate of Howe High School. She holds a B.A. degree from Indiana University, a certification in social work from Clark Atlanta University, and a master's in counseling from Indiana State University.

Tracy works for the Indianapolis Public School System and is an assistant professor at Indiana State University. She is the co-founder of Be Free Indy, a nonprofit organization for human trafficking awareness.

Tracy's passion to empower girls and young women has led to the start of several mentoring groups. As a counselor, she started several groups, including the Girls to Women Mentoring Program and the Academic Success Program.

Tracy holds numerous civic roles and responsibilities throughout central Indiana. She has received several awards and acknowledgments for her outstanding professional and community involvement.

Tracy is also a licensed minister, serving at Living Water Fellowship Church of Indianapolis, IN, under the senior teachers and administrators Pastors Steve and Kim Outlaw.

Tracy is an avid learner who enjoys fashion, traveling, and giving back to the community. In her spare time, she enjoys spending time with her friends and family.

Tracy is married to Dale R. Pruitt and is the mother of four adult children and a teenage son.

CHAPTER ONE

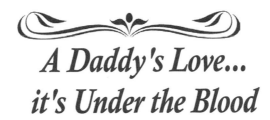

A Daddy's Love...
it's Under the Blood

JUST MY IMAGINATION

My first encounter with him was at the end of my bed. Standing at the end of the bed with those long ponytails. Ponytails as thick as a braided rope sharing the same color of red Georgia clay. I was waiting to talk to her but He invaded my space. Who was this person talking? It was not the voice of Teisha. I wanted to have a conversation with Teisha. We had a lot to talk about; kindergarten was tough. Teisha was my imaginary friend and I was expecting to talk to her that evening. But someone else decided to come in the room. It was a man with authority. He stopped me in my tracks. Although his voice was strong, I felt his love. The love in his voice went through the soul of my long, skinny body. Looking through the murky water of the fish tank beyond that bright orange coral reef I heard very clearly.

"I am going to use you," He said.

With a sassy voice I answered, "Who is this talking?"

"It's me, daughter, I am going to use you," He said.

"God is that you?" I asked.

"Yes," He said.

"What are you talking about? I don't talk to you. I talk to Teisha," I replied.

At the tender age of five I heard him and the connection was real. Because of my vivid imagination, and the fact that no one other than my sister would entertain the thought that Teisha was real, and my mama said I had an imagination out of this world, I decided to keep this conversation to myself. Although I went to church every Sunday I didn't know God talked and would answer my questions. Yes, that is the first time I heard the voice of God. John 10:27(NLT) *My sheep listen to my voice; I know them, and they follow me.*

Isn't She Lovely

As a child, I was blessed. I was a daddy's girl in every sense of the word. I was my father's world. Likewise, he was mine. I was the youngest of four; however, I was his only child. I was a late-life baby, the accident, wasn't-supposed-to-be-here-at-all baby. My sisters were so in love with me, and after the initial shock, I became my disgruntled brother's favorite little sidekick.

But my father doted over me. The lyrics of "Isn't She Lovely" by Stevie Wonder describes his love for me. Although I didn't grow up in the house with my daddy, not a day went by that he didn't confess his admiration for me. His love for me gave me security and helped me to display a great deal of confidence. This confidence made me wise before my time. At a young age, I became an innovative thought leader. My daddy helped me to believe I could do and be anything I set my mind to be.

My mother honed in on these gifts and began to cultivate them in my early years. I was involved in everything from playing the violin to modeling. My mother made sure my father financed all of my interests. He loved me so much he didn't care. Anything for his Lynne, the name he so affectionately called me. I never wanted to disappoint him so I excelled in school. My clothing mirrored his impeccable style for fashion. I kept my hair bows straight and patent leather shoes shined. I was well-spoken, bold, boisterous, and a risk-taker. He got a kick out of this. This behavior warmed his heart. He and my brother both loved my antics and both of them gave me their undivided attention. I had healthy relationships with the two most important men in my life. I shared my dreams and my fears with my father because he never judged me. He was a safe place. Although my father didn't attend church regularly he constantly reminded me that all his earthly treasures were because of God's love and grace. He taught me about tithing at the age of eight. He also taught me the law of reciprocity. It was these lessons that started me in giving and understanding the importance of advancing the Kingdom of God. I quickly learned that I was the apple of his eye, but more importantly the apple of God's eye. The foundation gave me confidence that I could ask God for anything because I was not scared to ask my daddy. That confidence would soon fade in the backdrop of my life, not returning for a long time.

Down but not Destroyed

It was a hot, humid summer morning. The sun was beating so hard, pushing its way through the pale blue custom drapes. Drapes that were closed to keep the heat out and the cool air in. Those pale blue drapes also trapped the chilling secret that would begin in that house. The room was filled with the scent of fresh lemon Pledge furniture cleaner. Yet the environment of the house was stale and cold.

Then it happened. The event that would change the trajectory of my life. I was in the home of a male relative. He told me to come into his bedroom. In a matter of minutes, he coerced me to take off my clothes. My innocence stripped off as each piece of clothing was removed. I became vulnerable when he told me to come into his room. It was that day I learned vulnerability caused me pain and harm. I made up my mind I would never let my guard down again.

Forgiveness was the fuel that drove me into my purpose.

🌿

I lost trust for all men on that summer day. Although I remained talkative, that was the day I lost my voice. The voice of confidence, the voice of security, the voice of belonging and the voice of joy, just to name a few. This one event that took less than fifteen minutes cost me nearly fifteen years to regain my voice.

I was repeatedly molested throughout the summer and each time a piece of my confidence went away. By the end of the summer I was a different person. Being rejected, abused, and misused I believed if my siblings found out I would be rejected by them.

Because of my fear, I literally lived two different lives within my ninety-five-pound body.

He convinced me that I had to keep the secret. My mother was dealing with her own health issues, and I refused to do anything that would send her into renal failure. After all, God had answered our prayers and she had received a kidney. I made a vow, I would not be the cause of her getting sick again. I definitely was not telling my father. My abuser warned me that my father would be angry with me and I would be in trouble. I never would do anything to lose my father's love. I buried the secret in the tear-filled brown carpet each time that I was violated. The lies of my attacker changed the way I viewed my father. I no longer looked at my daddy as an ally or advocate. He was now my father, the authoritarian that would punish me if he found out. So I made sure that I appeared as close to perfect as possible. That relative moved away at the end of summer, leaving my world in a turmoil. Afraid that someone would find out my secret, I worked hard to keep all eyes off me. I tried to live a perfect life on the outside while slowly dying on the inside. I continued to get good grades and used school as my outlet. I was active in school activities and one of the most popular girls in school.

I began smoking marijuana to numb the pain on the inside. Coercing a cousin to smoke with me and experimenting with alcohol with my best friend. I was a mess on the inside, even these two had no clue with what I was dealing with. I kept up the façade, because my grades were excellent.

At the age of 16 my mother passed away. Another part of me died. Once again I felt rejected. I was so angry she left me to live with this secret. At the time I was too young to realize it was not on purpose, but it was a large part of my purpose. It was at my mother's funeral that I was filled with the Holy Ghost, with the evidence of speaking in tongues. Yeah at a good ol' Baptist church. It was not until later in life that I would understand that I needed the Holy Ghost to keep me through what was to come. The power of the Holy Ghost would become my keeper.

I continued to excel in school, but I started looking for someone to replace my mother's love. I had my drugs to stabilize my pain but I became needy for a male's attention. After all, I had distanced myself from my father due to the shame. My mother was no longer there and I was still afraid to reach out to my siblings, thinking they would blame me. For the next fourteen years I looked for love and revenge for the things that I had endured. The blessing was that God never turned his back on me and the Holy Ghost still remained my guide.

Soon I had another drug: sexual promiscuity. I had learned sex and intimacy the wrong way so I acted accordingly. That first encounter was violent and painful, and my feelings about sex and intimacy were wrongfully based on that experience. I was determined I would never let another man hurt me.

In the back of my mind and deep in my heart the lyrics by Rick James and Teena Marie, *Fire and Desire* became my mantra. "Love them and leave them." That would be my claim to fame. I was on a quest to be a living black widow spider. I refused to be vulnerable to another man. I would make every one of my partners pay for what happened to me. However, through every encounter I would hear this voice saying "I have better for you." Sometimes this voice was loud and sometime is was still, but I always felt safe when it spoke. The voice of God. No matter where I was and my state of mind, He was there to comfort me.

I went to college studying interior and fashion design, determined to make a life for myself in New York. During summer school I was walking near the Sample Gates on Indiana University's campus and I heard a small voice say the same thing that I heard when I was five.

"I am going to use you. I'm going to use your pain. Your work is with children."

I sat down on a bench. I spoke back to the voice saying, "I don't even like kids." I spent the rest of my summer wrestling with what I heard, but determined not to tell my friends because they'd think I was crazy. The fall of my junior year I changed my major and stopped pursing an internship with the fashion house of Calvin Klein. I also stopped smoking marijuana for about six months because I thought it was making me hear things. It was at that time that I threw myself in my new classes and never looked back on what I thought I was losing. Despite my new classes and all that I was learning about trauma, I continued to live with that nasty secret that haunted me.

Three Beauties for Ashes

In the midst of trying to figure out what to do with this new normal, God blessed me with a beautiful baby girl a couple of months before graduation. This was the first time I felt a real since of joy since that horrible summer. I had no clue what to do with this perfect doll, yet I knew she depended on me and I would do whatever I needed to protect her. I remember asking God, "Please take care of her because I am a mess."

She was a breath of fresh air. My daddy felt a whole new connection to me. She filled the distance that was forged. I remember he looked at her and doted over her like he did me, a reminder of what once was. Three years later, working in my career, still struggling to make sense of my life I gave birth to another baby girl. She was a complete clone of me. Once again, my father doted and puffed out his chest. He was the proudest grandfather and father. His life was perfect and we grew so close. I realized I needed him and he was there every time I called on him. But his tone was changing. Our conversations began to shift. He constantly reminded me of God's grace and goodness. He told me that I needed to trust in God and not him. Reminding me of Romans 2:4 (NLT) *Don't you see how wonderfully kind, tolerant, and patient God is with you? Does this mean nothing to you? Can't you see that his kindness is intended to turn you from your sin?*

Something was changing. My father was giving me very clear instructions. It was at this time that I rededicated my life to the Lord. I truly started to seek a real and true relationship with God. I started working in the church and then, three months later, my father died.

Isaiah 26:3(NLT) *You will keep in perfect peace all who trust in you, all whose thoughts are fixed on you!* became rhema to me. I had a peace that shocked me and everyone else.

My father's funeral was a blur. However, I remember a woman coming up to me and saying in my ear, "God is going to send you another man to love you just like Christ loved the church. He is going to love you and you will be vulnerable to his love."

After the funeral, I questioned my friends and other family members about this lady. No one saw her at the funeral or noticed her whispering in my ear. I know what I saw and heard and I stood on that conversation.

I decided to relocate to the south, moving with no job, two children and $120 in my pocket. With limited resources, I realized for the first time in my life I only had God to depend on. God blessed me with a jovial baby boy. His innocence and minor breathing problems drew me even closer to the Lord. I began to pray, read, and study my bible. My faith increased as I learned about the promises of God. I watched God heal my son from Asthma. I begin to know God as a healer. Through the eyes of these three beautiful children I saw that I needed more. I started not only attending church but living his word. The word was changing my life and the cycle of my self-destructive behavior. I sat in Sunday school listening to a lesson being taught on forgiveness. "Unforgiveness will eat you up like cancer," my Sunday school teacher said. Those words went through my soul.

I went home and dropped to my knees crying out to God. I begged God for the strength to forgive my relative and to truly forgive myself. It felt like one hundred pounds of bricks fell off my back. I was a new person. I heard the same voice that I heard as a five-year-old. "You must call him and tell him you forgive him and you release him," God told me. "Your reward will be so great." I obeyed God and although my molester denied any wrongdoing. I believed God that my reward would be great.

Restoration

Forgiveness was the fuel that drove me into my purpose. As, I grew in the word of God I begin to get an understanding of God's redemptive power. I moved from victim to a place of victory, recognizing that my life had purpose. More importantly, my natural father was no longer my god. I embraced a daddy's love from my eternal father. God did for me what my biological father could not do; He delivered me and restored me. God restored my voice and confidence. I gained a new determination to be the best I could be in the Lord. I answered my call to the ministry and worked hard to lead the lost to the Kingdom of God.

It's Under the Blood

Wanting the people I loved to share my new found love for the Lord, I came to Indianapolis for a week-long visit. It was then that I met the love of my life, my husband. From the moment we met, I felt a sense of security and acceptance. The sassy voice of that little five-year-old said to him, "I'm going to be vulnerable with you. I have never been this vulnerable. I need to tell you my story. If we are going to do life together you need to know this." I was truthful, I was vulnerable, and not ashamed of my past.

He listened; his words were few but strong. "It is under the blood." Those five words dried up a decade worth of drenching sorrow. The trajectory of my life was again changed. This time for the better. His unconditional love for me challenges me to be the innovative thought leader that was buried as a girl. He is my biggest cheerleader rooting me to victory and coaching me during setbacks. His determination to live the scripture, Ephesians 5:25 (NLT) *For husbands, this means love your wives, just as Christ loved the church. He gave up his life for her,* gives me the confidence to keep my eyes and ears open to Gods' purpose and voice.

I want to take this time to encourage you to give God every hurt, disappointment, mishap, and mistake to him. Allow God to heal you, set you free and restore you to your place of purpose. You are here because you have the victory. Your purpose is bigger than your pain.

And I am convinced that nothing can ever separate us from God's love. Neither death nor life, neither angels nor demons¹ neither our fears for today nor our worries about tomorrow — not even the powers of hell can separate us from God's love. Romans 8:38. God wants to get glory out of your life and all that you have experienced, the good, bad and the ugly. Open your eyes, ears, and heart to your Daddy's love. Be vulnerable to him. Let God show himself strong in the midst of it all.

Endnotes
John 10:27(NLT)
Romans 2:4 (NLT)
Isaiah 26:3(NLT)
Ephesians 5:25 (NLT)
Romans 8:38 (NLT)

Crystal Moore

Crystal Moore has a passion to share the love of God with others and to use her personal testimony of God's grace actively working in her life, to encourage as many people as she possibly can.

Crystal was born and raised in Terre Haute, Indiana and currently resides in Noblesville, Indiana. She has been married to her husband, Martel Moore for 15 years and is the mother of Rramaj, Nevaeh, and Justice.

Crystal has enjoyed serving in ministry for the past 12 years as youth pastor, mentor, teacher, missionary, and intercessor. She is currently working alongside her husband, Martel helping to operate and manage a small marketing company in Indianapolis, In.

Crystal is also the founder of Run 4 Life, an organization established to encourage women on their journey of healthy living. The goal of Run 4 Life is to bring together a community of women to work toward a common goal of enhancing our health: spirit, soul, and body.

Crystal received her associates of science degree in human services and continues to seek opportunities to learn in the areas of self enhancement and leadership to help her better serve her community with her God given gifts and talents.

CHAPTER TWO

Beauty in Brokenness

My Brokenness Speaks...

If you cannot speak your brokenness your brokenness will speak for you. Pete Rollins
My emotions racing, my heart pounded as I pulled up my husband's Gmail account and scrolled through the emails. There it was, the personal phone number to one of his business partners. I noticed him on a couple former business trips; he was about ten years younger than myself: charismatic personality, kind of cocky, and very successful. I was attracted to him. There was something about him that intrigued me, a woman desperate and broken looking to ease the pain by any means necessary.

He worked closely with my husband and had just been to visit our office. We had few interactions alone but I knew in my mind that I wanted the association to go further. I was sick; sick in my mind and in my emotions. I knew it. I was honest with myself about what and why I was acting out in this way, but I had reached a point where a part of me just didn't care anymore. For once, it just felt good to do what felt good. It soothed my hurt even in just the fantasy of it all.

I took a deep breath, feeling so empowered by what I was about to do. The adrenaline reminded me that I was alive, when most of the time I felt dead inside in regards to my marriage and my life. I wanted to go beyond the fantasy and make it reality. I even considered the consequences I could expect to deal with when I followed through with my plan of sending that message and extending the invitation of myself to him.

I was experienced in life and self-medicating enough to know that deep down this really wasn't the answer. It was a temporary fix or at least what I hoped it would be, and in that moment, that was enough.

Bleeding....
Until you heal the wounds of your past, you will continue to bleed. Iyanla Vanzant

Taking a walk down memory lane isn't always a pleasant one. Especially when some of those paths you have taken whether willing or unwilling, have been dark, scary, and quite painful. Many of us would choose to only remember those paths that felt serene. We tend to suppress the darker parts of our story sometimes out of fear. I think at times maybe that is what we think is needed to protect our own sanity.

I believe that at some point, God asks us to allow him access to those deep, dark places because he knows what we don't. He knows that the pain, hurt, and trauma has the potential to eventually destroy us on the inside if not properly handled and ultimately healed. For God to heal our brokenness at the deepest level today, we must eventually revisit and face the painful places of yesterday.

As a teen, I placed myself into very risky and harmful situations, resulting in some horrible experiences. The destruction that comes with a promiscuous lifestyle especially for a 14 and 15 year old young girl can be utterly devastating. At the age of 14, I was involved in a mentally and physically abusive same-sex relationship. I drank alcohol, experimented with marijuana and became sexually active with grown men. It got so bad that I was drinking myself to the point of being so "out of it" (even unconscious at times) that men would take advantage of me to the point of raping me.

When I was 15 I met a boy around my age and we began a relationship that would last for about four years. Early on he had become emotionally, mentally, and physically abusive to me. We had a son together and when he was about five months old I was finally able to gain the courage to leave the relationship with his father.

My husband, Martel, was instrumental with helping me leave the abusive situation. We became friends working together, started to date sometime after, and we were married six months later. We were young and didn't understand the challenges we would face together, but deep inside both of us was a knowing that this was supposed to be. We could feel it, even over the fear of that life altering choice we made to get married at 19 and 20 years old.

Grace Calling...

Define yourself radically as one beloved by God, every other identity is an illusion. Brennan Manning

Even though we started attending church regularly and became very involved, I was so bound up by my past and ways of thinking I started to experience some pretty severe anxiety attacks. Things got worse before they got better, but it was during that time that I discovered the power in prayer, worship, and God's Word. I was delivered from the bondages of my past as well as the anxiety and fear. I began to learn how to take authority in my life through the active power of the Holy Spirit working in me.

After about three years we felt God leading us to a new church. After about a year of being at our new church we took a part-time position as staff youth pastors. We had services Wednesday night, did special youth events, youth conferences, fundraisers, etc. Our ministry seemed to be very effective, we were growing and it seemed life had never been better.

We began to take more responsibility in the church in addition to the youth. We were leading choir ministry, intercessory prayer, and anything extra that was going on. We were spending four to five days a week at the church not to mention by that time we had three young children and an adopted teenage son. Ministry seemed to always come first for both of us. Even when we tried to be aware and bring balance we would always put everything aside to make sure ministry was taken care of. We were burnt out and it was about to become evident that everything was not as good as at it appeared on the surface.

As we ended our third year as youth pastors I found out that my husband was having a sexually explicit text conversation with a girl in our youth group. There was a plan to go further but it was interrupted by her confession to me. I was shocked, devastated, and heartbroken by it all. I felt horrible for the girl, a girl I was attempting to mentor at the time. As awful as it all was, Martel and I began to work through it. I don't remember acting out in anger. I do remember being really hurt because of what it did to our ministry and concerned for the girl and how this would affect her as a person and her faith in God.

I am convinced that in the middle of our brokenness is where we meet Jesus and are introduced to grace...

We made it through the initial year of that "hit" and even renewed our vows celebrating 10 years of marriage. Things seemed to be really good between us and otherwise. During this time God began to speak to me about the message of grace, shaking me up regarding my own personal theology. God was delivering me from a works-based religion and teaching me how to rely fully on his grace. He was teaching me to focus on the power of the cross and his finished work rather than trying to obtain grace and favor through how "good" I was.

As I felt God speaking to me I eventually went to my pastors. I knew we would need to move on to a new church after the way they had responded and the conflict of beliefs. As a consequence to our parting, our friends and church family were steered away from us by the leadership.

I was devastated deep within my soul. As time went on I came face to face with all of the feelings from my husband's indiscretions on top of my feelings of abandonment from those in the church whom I considered my family. I was left to deal alone. It seemed every person in my life that I considered close were no longer there. It became hard to trust, I became very cynical about the church and I began isolating myself. The enemy had come at me with everything he could. His intention was to steal, kill, and destroy me and my family and I was on the verge of letting him do just that.

Grace > Sin

Sin does not stop God's grace from flowing but God's grace will stop sin. Joseph Prince

As a Christian, sin is in direct conflict to what our true nature (our Christ nature) desires. I had turned to sin in an attempt to dull the pain because I had lost something vital over those past five years. Among many things, I had lost hope. Hope in people, and ultimately hope in God. With that hope diminishing so followed my identity and purpose.

God was grieved because of it all. I could feel it in the depths of my heart. He was grieved not because we hadn't followed through with obeying his laws, or because we were an embarrassment to him, or because we failed to set an example of what a good Christian looks like. No, He was grieved because his children were broken. I could hear Him calling me to come to him. I could hear Him telling me that I didn't have anything to prove or explain. I could feel his unconditional love. Not because I was worthy by my own merit or even because I would choose the "right thing." He wasn't manipulating me so that I would do something, he was just loving me simply because he loved me.

That kind of love gave me power; power to choose what I felt in my heart his spirit was leading me to. He was leading me and inviting me to trust him, in and through the process of healing. He wasn't asking me to make a commitment or pinky swear to promises I didn't know if I could keep. He was just asking me in that moment, to simply look to him.

Religion gives way for resentment when we are motivated to do the right thing from a place of religious obligation. We will end up resenting God and those **we say** we forgive and love. When we are motivated by love, the outcome will always be victory.

In the middle of the pain and in the middle of the process grace is being fully realized. At our most broken places is when we are most aware of how abundant it is and how truly amazing it is. Grace is not us trying to make something happen by our own ability and strength. When it comes to our process of transformation. Grace is the person of Jesus working in us and our yielding to that process. We yield by faith and faith comes by hearing the words of Christ.

Broken and Beautiful...

To be alive is to be broken, and to be broken is to stand in the need of grace. Brennan Manning

I remember when I first reached out for someone other than my husband. He was sold out to God-single, a man after God's heart. I think that is what initially attracted me to him. I had created this getaway in my mind with him for months before I reached out to him through Facebook message. I had not done anything like this or even thought to since I rededicated my life to the Lord in my early twenties. I was now 34 years old and I was at a clear breaking point. The audacity of me, I could hardly believe it myself but my brokenness was manifesting and it couldn't be any more evident.

When we are motivated by love, the outcome will always be victory.

You would have thought that maybe there would have been a sense of evening the score but by that point I didn't ultimately want revenge. I just wanted out. I wasn't satisfied and there was a war going on the inside between who I was and who I (my flesh) wanted to be. I was tired of doing the right thing, tired of being taken for granted. I was done and I didn't want to be sorry. Still the conflict inside remained and the thoughts had already taken on a life of their own.

This was the reality I had chosen because it seemed the better alternative to my actual reality. From what I could tell, through the cynicism that blurred my perspective doing the "right thing" was reciprocated by being lied to, cheated on, heartbroken, and abandoned. Talk about becoming weary in well doing. I was beyond weary. I had moved from weary to mad, and bitter. Bitter at my husband, bitter at all the people in my life who I thought loved me but were clearly no longer a part of my life. I was bitter at God for allowing these things to happen over the past five years. After all, how was any good coming from all I had endured? I couldn't see it and I didn't understand. It's one thing when you go through trials and you can see how God is using them to bless people and to draw people to himself, but when you feel your suffering is in vain it can quickly cause you to lose heart. It can cause you to lose faith in the ONE you know has always been there.

I was fed up and I went to God angry about it all, angry about how he could even expect me to stay after everything I had dealt with. Marriage is not easy even when you calculate all the things a couple deals with minus the infidelity. Those problems alone are more than enough to make a person want to quit. I wanted to know how any of this was fair to me. Why did I always have to be the bigger person, why did I always have to do what was right? Why did I have to bear THIS STORY and feel the anguish of its effects? Once I was done saying all I wanted to say, I got quiet enough to listen.

He said, it's not fair, daughter. It's not. However, it was necessary for your growth, for his growth and for my will to be accomplished. There is a space that you meet with me that can't be known but through personal pain and trauma. You have known me more because of it and you will know me more as you let me walk you through it. You will know me, and you will know yourself.

I remember one day talking to my husband about how I felt. I told him I didn't want to be with him anymore. I felt no desire to make it work though I felt guilty for not wanting it to, it was my truth and I couldn't be anything but honest. I was dying inside.

At one point, my husband looked at me with tears in his eyes and said "This isn't you Crystal, this isn't who you are." He proceeded to tell me that he took full responsibility and that he knew that his actions were what had brought me to this place.

I had turned to self-destructive behavior trying to numb my pain through relationships outside of my marriage. It had become a serious addiction in my mind. I entertained fantasies and eventually those thoughts manifested into action that led to me reaching out through messages and phone calls. Two conversations with my husband's coworker were fortunately as far as it went, but opened a door that was rather difficult to close because the pictures I had created in my mind were being reinforced and catering to my very real emotions. Our mind is powerful! I was so careless of my thoughts because of my brokenness that those thoughts built up strongholds that were not so easily destroyed.

Though I knew my husband's apologies were genuine, sometimes my heart wouldn't allow me to be receptive. There were times I couldn't even accept his sincerity for the overshadowing of his past failures. Other times I could feel my heart overflowing with gratitude and welcoming his words of love and hope for our marriage to have life again. It was in those times I was reminded that God was working. I was reminded that there's still hope for me and that healing is taking place even if it's just a little at a time. I'm reminded that grace is greater than my sin. I'm reminded that grace is a person and his name is Jesus.

Seeing God in the Midst...

I now see how owning our story and loving ourselves through that process is the bravest thing that we will ever do. Brene' Brown

One of the things I have learned throughout this journey is that life isn't black and white. Each of us has a different story. Some of our stories are similar but the details are sacred, personal, and unique to each one of us. Our outcomes may vary but no matter where our journey has brought us to at this point one thing is certain, God is with us! He is leading us and guiding us. Sometimes he's carrying us when it all seems too much. I firmly believe that God is continually extending a personal invitation to exchange the ashes of our lives for the beauty of redemption.

If I'm honest I'm afraid. Afraid of allowing myself to be uncertain. I am afraid of not having it all figured out. I'm learning that relinquishing that fear and control to God is a key to walking in faith and allowing God's grace to work effectively.

Trusting God to walk me through my pain, to heal me and restore me some days is enough and the uncertainties in those times don't mean as much. I remember days when I felt I was falling apart I would hear my seven-year-old daughter Justice asking me "How did you and Daddy meet?" and God reminding me of the divine plan that he brought together 15 years ago. I hear hope in my 12-year-old daughter's (Nevaeh) laughter and I am reminded that God's love is greater than anything we face in this life. I look at my 15-year-old son (Rramaj) and admire his free spirit and playfulness no matter who's watching and I wonder if I could be like him one day, shedding myself of the need to please people. To rid myself of this overwhelming sense of need to be perfect.

Maybe as a human being and even more as a believer in the redeeming power of Christ, my need to see this whole thing put back perfectly packaged right now is precisely the reason why it can't be. Maybe if the picture of victory came too soon, I would miss out on the beauty in this broken place. Just maybe, the redemption, the place of victory as we envision it would not taste as sweet if we didn't first experience the pain within the process.

Is it possible that I had to endure betrayal by those closest to me so that I could experience a glimpse of glory in the reality of forgiveness, love and grace?

A Glimpse of Glory...

I am certain of this; I have seen the face of God and looked into his eyes like I never could before. No shame, no fear, just his eyes looking into mine with great love for me, for my husband, and for all of broken humanity. It didn't matter anymore the depth of my broken, sinful, disobedient acts. In that moment I understood when I looked into his eyes how deep and how wide his love was for me, bringing me to my knees at the powerful reality that, that is enough.

I realized that at the root of it all my husbands' brokenness had nothing to do with me. That was something God wanted to deal with. The sin that brought it all to light for us to see may have just been grace working. Grace beckoning for him to come and be held, to be healed from the abuse and dysfunction of his own childhood.

Is it possible that God honors us in these broken places, to taste of the sorrow Jesus himself endured on our behalf?

He was despised and rejected a man of sorrows acquainted with deepest grief. Isaiah 53:3

Is it possible that we experience him and relate with him in the midst of our broken places?

I am convinced that in the middle of our brokenness is where we meet Jesus and are introduced to grace lest we forget how amazing it truly is.

Whenever, though, they turn to face God as Moses did, God removes the veil and there they are — face to face! They suddenly recognize that God is a living, personal presence, not a piece of chiseled stone. And when God is personally present, a living spirit, that old, constricting legislation is recognized as obsolete. We're free of it! All of us! Nothing between us and God, our faces shining with the brightness of his face. And so we are transfigured much like the Messiah, our lives gradually becoming brighter and more beautiful as God enters our lives and we become like him. 2 Corinthians 3:18 MSG

<u>Endnotes</u>

Psalm 73:26

Romans 8:37-39NLT

Psalm 34:18 NLT

2 Corinthians 12:9 NLT

Romans 5:19-21 NLT

2 Timothy 1:7 NLT

1 Peter 5:8 NLT

1 Corinthians 13:7-8

2 Corinthians 10:5 NIV

Romans 12:2 NLT

Philippians 3:12 MSG

Romans 5:20-21 MSG

Devon L. Holifield, Sr.

Minister Devon L. Holifield, Sr. is a leader, life coach, and author. Born in Indianapolis, Indiana, on April 16, 1991, he is happily married to Shaneece Holifield; both agree that their best accomplishment is their children Zariyah, Devon Jr., and Christian. Minister Holifield was baptized on July 4, 2010.

He confesses it was divine nature that the day our nation celebrates independence, he became dependent on God. In 2011, God led Minister Holifield to the Rock Full Gospel Ministries, with a mindset to start over and take the works of God seriously. Under numerous hours and training with Pastor Jerome Taylor, he began to grow spiritually and mentally. As the year went by, Min. Holifield accepted his calling to the ministry. In November 2013, Pastor Jerome Taylor officially licensed Devon Holifield as an associate minister of the Rock Full Gospel Ministries.

In June 2016, he successfully completed the certification in the 5D Coach Program with Authentic Identity Institute. Min. Holifield is a graduate of the Luke 418 Ministerial Training Academy. Currently, he is a student of the Southern Theological Institute of Biblical Studies (STIBS) pursuing his dual bachelors' degree due to graduate in the summer of 2018.

CHAPTER THREE

Destined For Greatness

When you are destined for greatness, you are operating in your purpose. The fulfillment to know that God designed a destiny for you is one thing, but many of us go about life not fulfilling it. We sacrifice the greatness we are destined for, for family, a stable career, and other circumstances. I'm willing to compromise many things, but we should never compromise our destiny. We must make sure that we are operating in our purpose, on purpose. When we do not, things begin to be too uncomfortable to bear. We put ourselves up against situations that we were not designed to defeat. For example, we all have our own giants that we have the victory over. However, I could not win against Goliath because Goliath was David's victory. Instead, we must be in alignment for the assignment. My purpose is not to battle your trials and tribulations, only my own. On your journey to greatness, you may notice that other people are more focused on themselves instead of pursuing their destiny.

Being destined for greatness demands attention and discipline. Just like gathering ingredients to make the perfect pound cake, choose the right ingredients for your destiny. It would be extremely disheartening to know you never reached your destiny simply because you added someone or something into the recipe that did not belong. We must be careful of the decisions we make, for our destiny depends on it. Some people come along that look as if they would be good ingredients but are toxic to your recipe for destiny. Through fervent prayer and revelation, God shows us those we ought to associate with. Sometimes we come to a point of clarity and realize some people, the ones we thought had our back, do more damage than helping us. We cannot have a passive attitude when encountering people like this. When God shows you those who need to leave your life and you still choose to be connected to the individual, you are flirting with GreatLESSness. There is with no question, a destiny for you to fulfill. The question is more dependent on your perception to believe. There is no comparison to your greatness, because everyone has their own. Being destined for greatness comes with great responsibility, you need to be fully devoted and disciplined in order to come full term with the greatness within you.

The Struggle Is Real

In order to move towards your destiny, you have to face the fact that the struggle is real. Today, we often use this as a cliché to express various hardships in our lives. Struggling with the burdens to raise six kids by yourself as a single parent, facing unemployment in a difficult economy, or whatever goal you are trying to achieve, you must recognize that there will be some type of struggle. You can only defeat the opposition if you face that it actually exists. When you fear your struggles, your struggles consume you. When you face your struggles, you overcome them! Not recognizing the realness of every struggle you experience can be potentially harmful to yourself and others.

How, do you ask? Well, because struggles are required to survive in life. In order to stand up, you have to know what falling down is like. I once found myself homeless for many months. Prior to being homeless, I did not know what it was like. Imagine being locked in a room the size of a prison cell, for about three months. My family consisted of my pregnant fiancé, and our wonderful daughter who was a toddler at the time. While I may not have been incarcerated physically, I was stressed from the pains of mental incarceration. I had to experience not knowing where I was going to lie down for the evening, and having to buy ice to put in a cooler so my fiancé and I could feed our daughter while she was pregnant with my son; I didn't fully understand the issue at hand until life slapped me in the face with it. I was unemployed, receiving only seventy-seven dollars a week. One of the most difficult times in my life. I would have been fine by myself to be honest. However, when you have a family depending on you, there is no room for mistakes. You have no other option than to operate in the greatness that God has given you. It is absolutely mind-blowing to know that the struggle I was in was developing the strength I needed for today. Now, I understand the importance and the severity to never allow my family or myself to experience that again. There is no shame in talking about it; in fact, I thank God for sending me such a message that taught me a valuable lesson that cannot be learned in school. Sometimes it takes an overwhelming breakdown to have an undeniable breakthrough. You were given this life because you are strong enough to live it. The truth is that all life demands some type of struggle. Those who have everything given to them can become lazy, selfish, and insensitive to the real values of life.

Trust in His plan, not your pain

Every struggle in your life has shaped and/or will shape you into the person you are today. It teaches us what God wants us to know, to help us achieve what he has designed for us. There are many stories and lessons in the Bible about struggling. Take Job for example, what person can really say that they have struggled more than he has? The Lord allowed the enemy to mess with Job so much that he started to despair life within him. His friends accused him of falling out of grace with God, his spouse told him to offend and curse God, and he never found out why the Lord allowed him to suffer so much loss. He lost many things and people, including his wealth, his children, his health, his livestock and crops, and finally his marriage. He probably felt like he was God's enemy because of his severe suffering and therefore started complaining to the Lord about his conditions. Please

32

understand, and come to terms that Job really struggled and suffered a lot. He even stated "I loathe my very life; therefore, I will give free rein to my complaint and speak out in the bitterness of my soul. I say to God, 'Do not declare me guilty, but tell me what charges you have against me. Does it please you to oppress me, to spurn the work of your hands, while you smile on the plans of the wicked?'"

Have you ever felt like that? Have you ever asked similar questions? Well I guarantee that you are not alone. The Lord understands, he knows how we feel and how much pain we are in. I believe that in certain periods of our life, we begin to question Him. Sometimes I have even gotten to a point to doubt Him, but in my doubting of God…he restored my faith, and I learned to never do it again.

The point is, nobody is immune to the struggle. In fact, the more you struggle, the more respect you are positioned to receive. Not only does it matter how much you struggle, but also the act of embracing your struggle must take place as well. Your struggle means nothing if you are a victim of it. Bishop Paul S. Morton, the founder of the Full Gospel Baptist Church Fellowship endured one of the worst struggles in history. In August 2005, Hurricane Katrina demolished the southern United States with historic damage, devastating many states in particular the southern states of Louisiana, Texas, Mississippi and Georgia. He endured this disaster and survived a battle with colon cancer. Today, he is widely known as one of the wisest and admired bishops in the world. Not because he served faithfully at so many capacities. It is because his integrity was put to the test! He has been through the fire, and he overcame in the trials of adversity. Our scars are evidence of the struggle, but the good news is they are indicators of where we have been. They are not dictators of where we are going.

Be Aware, That You Are Rare

Being destined for greatness is not all too common in today's world. Usually, our definition of greatness is not all too positive. Reality TV stars and corrupt politicians are what come to mind when some of us think of greatness. I believe that it is safe to say that being destined for true greatness is very rare. The definition of rare means to be unusually great! We must comprehend with the fullest intentionality to be aware that we are rare.

In the Bible, 1 Peter 2:9-10 states, *But you are a chosen generation, a royal priesthood, a holy nation, his own special people, that you may proclaim the praises of him who called you out of darkness into his marvelous light; who once were not a people but are now the people of God, who had not obtained mercy but now have obtained mercy.* This scripture lets us know how much God thinks about us. When you begin to know your worth, you will not give people discounts. Because when you are rare, your value increases. The demand on your quality increases. I am aware that I am rare because your opinion does not determine my reality. I am rare because I am not going to fit in with everyone. I also know the great ones never do. I am rare because no one can change who God intended for me to be! Being aware that you're rare, is a pre-requisite for your greatness.

It's Time to Come Out!

When you are destined for greatness, coming out of your current situation is one of the most challenging things to do. David was known as a man after God's own heart, and he was indeed destined for greatness. He collided with a time in his life where he hit rock bottom. The bad news about being at rock bottom is that you are at rock bottom. The good news is that the situation cannot get any worse and the only way to go is to ascend, descending is no longer an option. While in the Cave of Adullam, David went through the process to become the next king. When you are destined for greatness, you will have some cave experiences. Have you ever found yourself in a cave? Not a real physical cave, but a cave of despair and despondency where the darkness seems to swallow you up? God does some of his best work in those cave experiences. These cave experiences can be used to your advantage to catapult you into your destiny. We all have a season where we are in our cave; the blessing in the cave is you will come out of it.

It's A Fixed Fight

Being destined for greatness is a fixed fight. A fight of Faith, Integrity, Grace, Humility and Triumph. Advertising agencies and marketing psychologists have known for years the power that seeing and messaging play in persuading consumers to buy their products. Every year billions of dollars are spent on creative and unique television commercials, all aimed at your brain and your wallet. Whether it is for the latest pair of Jordan gear or for a bowl of cereal, which makes you Coo-Coo for Cocoa Puffs.... consumers are bombarded with strategic messaging, in every form of media that exists. Advertising companies know that what we see and what we hear can make our imaginations go crazy in just a few seconds.

The enemy also understands that if he manipulates your senses, he can manipulate your perception. Goliath got into the hearts and minds of the children of Israel and messed up their imagination, telling them morning and night for forty days what he was going to do and what they could not do. He had so many weapons he needed an armor bearer to carry his shield. Yet, the Israelites were too scared to think, "If Goliath is supposed to be such a champion, why does he need that many weapons?"

Obedience is the key to unlock the components of being destined for greatness.

When people are not really about that life, they put on a front in order to scare other people.

For those of you who are boxing fanatics, you will remember that Mike Tyson went into the ring wearing no socks. He was breaking the protocol because this was not normal. In the ring, he wore no fancy robe, no socks, and many have reported no underwear either! Unlike Goliath, it was Tyson's unique fighting technique, and not what he wore that did all the talking when the fight was on. A real God-ordained champion does not have to have on a lot of stuff. What makes you a heavyweight champion is that you are able to fight when you have nothing. You can knock out circumstances and people that surround you because they underestimate you. They are judging you based on what you have or do not have. Those who are hating on you, those who are jealous of you, or lying on you don't understand what makes you a champion is that God is with you! It is amazing how God, through our own life experiences, is preparing us for our divine purpose. Oftentimes, God introduces us to a particular situation so that He can set us up for our destiny. God may not call you through a star in the night sky, a burning bush, or an upper room experience. Nevertheless, God can send you to complete a seemingly normal task that will trigger His master plan for your life. When you are destined for greatness, remember that every battle is a fixed fight in your favor.

Trust In His Plan, Not Your Pain

My most favorite scripture is *Keep my commands in your heart, for they will prolong your life many years and bring you peace and prosperity. Let love and faithfulness never leave you; bind them around your neck, write them on the tablet of your heart. Then you will win favor and a good name in the sight of God and man. Trust in the LORD with all your heart and lean not on your own understanding; in all your ways submit to him, and he will make your paths straight.* Proverbs 3:1-6 (NIV).

Solomon writes some heavy words that puts us in a divine perspective in how we operate in our faith. It is essentially important, because as he knew, there will be many times in our walk that we will come across situations that make us doubt what God is doing, especially when we are struggling. I don't think it is a coincidence this scripture is found in what is known as the Book of Wisdom by theologians. Every command that God gives us is a mandatory order. It is so important, that God tells us to keep them in our heart. Because He knows that in our lives, our decisions are often made based on the contents of our minds rather than the contents of our hearts. We all want to be destined for greatness, but not many of us know how to spell it. O-B-E-D-I-E-N-C-E.

Obedience is the key to unlock the components of being destined for greatness. Your life will be prolonged because you were obedient and kept God's commands. Peace and prosperity are also benefits in which you will receive when his commands are kept. Love and faithfulness are essential characteristics in every believer. People who love not only feel it, but also act with love too. People of faith not only believe in faith, but also act in faith too! Then when these things have been properly completed, we will be rewarded favor and a good name in the sight of God *and man*. Pride and the lack of humility will not be an asset to anyone who is seeking favor from the Almighty. The sacrifices, the tribulations you have endured, the pain you have experienced will earn you favor from God!

While I believe that God will provide the steps you need to take, take heed, there is a mindset you have to possess in order to be destined for greatness. If you can trust in the Lord with all your heart and lean not to your own understanding, God will take you to places you have only dreamed about seeing. The prosperity meter on your life will become stuck at the highest level just by trusting in his plan and not your pain. When God knows that there is no limit to your faith, there is no limit to his blessings! You are destined for greatness, and when God shows you a glimpse of his Glory you have no other choice than to live life above "see" level. May God bless and keep you, by colliding your life with your destiny of greatness.

Endnotes:
1 Peter 2:9-10 NKJV
Proverbs 3:1-6 NIV

Tisha Sanders

Tisha Sanders is a woman with a heart chasing after God. Her passion is dancing for God, while ministering to His people in dance.

Tisha is a native of Dallas, Texas. She is the daughter of Elder Pete and Clarissa Harkless Sr. and the second oldest of three siblings. Tisha is the very proud mother of her beautiful flower, Simone Clair. She and her daughter currently reside in Indianapolis, Indiana.

Tisha graduated from Indiana Wesleyan University in Marion, Indiana where she obtained her bachelor of science degree in business management. She is currently working on her Masters of Business Administration with a concentration in healthcare management from Liberty University. Tisha proudly serves in the Indiana Army National Guard, where she is the Division Equal Opportunity Advisor.

She attends Umoja Christian Church in Indianapolis, IN, where she has been a dedicated member of the Divine Anointed Vessels in Dance (DAVID) Dance Ministry for the last nine years. She is a strong believer in God and in the power of dance-she believes that one can receive power, healing, deliverance, strength, forgiveness, and peace through the ministry of dance. Her quote, "I am a dancer; one of God's athletes".

CHAPTER FOUR

Living a Life Consumed by Fear

Have you ever been so afraid of something to the point where you allowed your fears to consume every part of your life? Have you been so afraid of living your life because you were so overcome with fear- fearful for your health, fearful of being alone and never getting married, fearful of death, fearful of being defeated in life, fearful of your financial status, just fear of living? It was more than fifteen years ago when I realized the spirit of fear had been consuming my entire life.

My Story

I remember the day so clearly. My alarm sounded at 6:15 AM. I awoke as I usually do when preparing for a morning flight. I quietly got ready for my four-day trip to the West Coast. I was being extra careful not to awaken my two roommates who had just got in earlier that morning from working a straight six-day trip. As I was in the bathroom putting on my makeup I heard a loud banging on the doors of my neighbors. The banging began downstairs, escalated upstairs, and eventually made its way to my door. As I answered the door to the abrupt banging and loud screaming voices, the cell phones of my roommates began ringing. I could not understand what everyone was so excited about or why everyone's phones were ringing, but I could sense that something was wrong, very wrong.

The landlord of my apartment building was frantic and overwrought! Upon opening my door, he began to shout, "Something is happening, something is happening!" Before I could inquire more about the distressed situation, I could hear and see that Sidney, one of my roommates, was on the phone with her mother. She was instructing her to turn on the television, as there was something very abnormal happening here. She stated there was a terrible accident and we all needed to get up and turn on the morning news. As I walked into the foyer of our apartment building I could see everyone from our building watching the news in tears and on their cell phones. They were all trying to contact their friends and family. At this point, I was still in a state of confusion. I had no idea what was going on until my roommate rushed over and grabbed me and stated a plane had crashed into the World Trade Center.

We originally and immediately thought there had to be a good explanation for this incident. We thought maybe the pilot had a heart attack, a stroke, or some type of ailment. As flight attendants, we all knew protocol and we all knew that planes were never allowed in that area; there was absolutely no reason for any plane to be that close. But to our dismay and astonishment, it was none of those things. It was far worse than any of us could have ever imagined. The United States was under attack and I was witnessing it first-hand. It was at that point when I realized I was beyond afraid. I was horrified! Every part of my being was consumed by fear. I desperately needed my parents. I needed to hear their voices. I needed to hear their words of comfort and reassurance that everything was going to be all right. I needed them to pray for me and all of us who were affected and touched by this calamity. As I stood there alone, afraid, and lost, it was at that moment when I realized I did not have a personal and intimate relationship with God for myself. I knew God, but I didn't know Him the way I needed to know Him.

God said, "Tisha, I have been here, I have always been here waiting for you"

Growing up in a Christian household, we were taught that whenever we felt afraid or we experienced negative emotions we should immediately begin to pray to God, the Holy One, for strength and a sound mind. How many times have you heard others say, during times of distress you should quote scriptures from the Bible? I have heard that more times than one. Being the daughter of a preacher and spending most of my life in church, I know that God has not given us the spirit of fear, but He has given us the spirit of love and of power and a sound mind. But at that moment, I could not think of one scripture. I had no verses to quote or prayers to mimic. I didn't call upon God the

Father, Son, or the Holy Spirit. I called upon my father, my birth father, because I knew that he knew who to call upon for me during these times of feeling distraught and perturbed. It was familiar to me and what I had always done during my times of trial and tribulation. It never became evident to me, until that day, that my birth father would one day leave me and I would have to know God for myself. Eventually, I would personally and directly have to call upon God for me and my household.

As I stood amongst many in the corridor of my apartment building, watching the breaking news relay information on what was taking place in New York City; my eyes began to well up with tears. Every person there was in tears and utter disbelief of what seemed to be a horror movie, but was very much our reality. I walked outside of my building and sat next to my roommate on the front steps. I will never forget the frightened look in her eyes as she asked me what were we going to do and how would we recover from something so horrific as this. She then burst into a bout of tears. As I put my arm around her, tears began to stream down my own face. I had no words of comfort for her, as I was trying to figure things out myself.

Overtaken by Fear

It was 10:05 AM and I was still unable to contact my mother or father. All lines were busy and no one had been allowed to leave their present locations. The governor had stated that we were now listed as being in a state of emergency and on lock down, meaning no one could leave or enter our locations. While sitting outside on the patio, looking out onto the Hudson

River I began to reminisce on the different events that had taken place over my life. I was so overwhelmed with fear. All I could think about were the times I had been afraid and how God intervened in my situation and turned things around. I thought about the time I joined the US Army. Many told me I would not make it. Others said I was too prissy and too feminine to be a member of Uncle Sam's Army. Their comments only made me want to join even more. Although I was timid and afraid of what was to come, I joined anyway and made it through successfully. It was only by God's grace and mercy that I made it through that challenging period of my life. *I can do all things through Christ who strengthens me.* Philippians 4:13.

When I decided to leave the military after four years, again I was frightened of what I could not see, the unknown. Everyone asked, "What are you going to do now? Do you have something lined up? You should just stay in. If it was me, I would be so afraid. You have it made here, why would you want to leave? What other job will allow you and your family to travel the world for free?" Well, I did it anyway. At the end of my tour I got out of the military, fearful of the unknown, but knowing that I had a prayer warrior praying for me and my well-being. My daddy, my mentor, my advisor and counselor was praying for me and with me.

The next stage of my life I was a twenty-four-year-old student working at MCI WorldCom advancing up the ladder in corporate America. One day while browsing the internet for new opportunities I came across an ad for a chance to work as a flight attendant for Continental Airlines. I thought to myself, why not? I arrived at the open call and was asked back for a second interview. Four interviews later, I found myself in Houston, Texas at an eight-week flight attendant training course. Again, I was overwhelmed with fear. This time, my fear was of failure; fear, that I wasn't good enough, fear that I did not have what it takes, fear of the unknown. Someone told me that I would have to change who I was if I wanted to make it in this career. But, guess what? I made it! God's word says, *He has not given us the spirit of fear.*

Looking out at the Hudson River, I could see submarines appear out of the water. I could see helicopters circling around us. I began to cry out to God, asking Him, why is this happening? I began to get angry because I was so afraid of the unknown. I was unable to speak with my safety net, my father. I could hear nothing from God, as He was silent. I walked to the front of my building where most of my neighbors had gathered. Some were inside of their apartments, discussing amongst each other their thoughts on what was going on. Others were conversing outside and watching with concern and disbelief of all the chaos that was taking place across the Hudson River in New York City.

The North Tower of the World Trade Center collapsed. We began to scream as tears rushed down our faces. One of the tenants fell to the ground as it was too much for her to bear; her mother worked inside of the World Trade Center and she had not been able to contact her since the event had taken place. I could not begin to imagine what she was going through at that moment. But, the three of us being there together and consoling one another was all we could do.

One of my roommates looked at me and said, "What are we going to do now? The other asked, isn't your father a preacher? Please ask him to pray for us, we need help here." I looked at her as helpless and perplexed as everyone else. I screamed, "I don't know what to do!" I called my father, but wasn't answering; no one was answering my calls or texts. I felt completely lost and utterly alone. But more than that, I felt embarrassed and ashamed. I thought of all the times that I had spent in Sunday School, Bible Study, Christian conferences, spiritual workshops, overnight prayers, etc. and I did not know how to directly reach out to God. I had to admit to myself that I did not have a real and personal relationship with God. How could this be? It was as if at that moment I had an epiphany, a moment of profound insight.

It is because of God that I can overcome my fears and emotional distress.

God said, "Tisha, I have been here; I have always been here, waiting for you." All this time I had been seeking God through my birth father; but my God, my Father, had always been there with His arms out stretched and waiting for me. Wow! He loves me that much. God loves us so much that He will wait for us until we realize how much we want Him and need Him; in the mean-time He consistently watches over us and protects us from hurt, harm, and danger. He loves us all that much.

Overcoming Fear

In Him is where I find peace and comfort. It is because of God that I can overcome my fears and emotional distress. I learned, to overcome my fears I must trust in God, read His word, and establish a personal relationship with Him. It would have been a contradiction for me to trust in God and yet remain consumed in fear. I could no longer allow fear to keep me from doing the will of God. Fear is not of God. So, if it is not of God, then it must be of Satan, another one of his tactics. *For God has not given us a spirit of fear, but of power and of love and of a sound mind.* 2 Timothy 1:7.

Looking at me, one would have never thought that I was living a life preoccupied by fear. But, this was my life. Have you ever heard the term, never judge a book by its cover?

It is because of God that I can overcome my fears and emotional distress.

Many have and are presently living and dealing with the same type of situation as I had been. Jehoshaphat was the king of Judah, (2 Chronicles, Chapter 20) and was yet living in fear at one point. Although it is in our human nature to be afraid, we must seek God and His Word for courage, a sound mind, encouragement, power, and reassurance. If we trust and believe God with our whole heart, He will remove all our fears and He will fight whatever it is that we are battling for us. My journey to seeking a personal relationship with God began that very moment, September 11, 2001 at 11:45 AM in Bayonne, New Jersey. I decided I was no longer going to allow the spirit of fear to consume me. I had made up my mind, I was going to seek God and live a life consumed by Him. For He is a God of love, power, peace, mercy, and understanding.

I decided I was no longer going to allow the spirit of fear to consume me. I had made up my mind, I was going to seek God and live a life consumed by Him.

It had been three days since we had seen the sun rise. At least that's how it felt. For three entire days, there were no flights, no driving, no laughter, and no hope for tomorrow (for some). Everyone was still in shock and disbelief of the turmoil that had taken place only a few days ago; but we knew we had to gather ourselves and prepare to move on with life. I remembered a bible verse that I would always revert to during my times of struggle; *I can do all things through Christ which strengthens me*, Philippians 4:13. This scripture has carried me throughout my entire adult life, and it did also that day. After everything had calmed down and life began to pick up again, I received the phone call.

It was 2:30 AM and I was still awake. I glanced over and both of my roommates were sound asleep. For the last three days, our days ended with at least two to three bottles of red wine consumed with whatever food we could find to munch on, as this was our means to making it through the day. I had my windows open and the curtains pulled back so that I could see and hear the waves of the Hudson River brush up against the banks. A week ago, those waves would have put me right to sleep. But since the attack on our country less than a week earlier, I hadn't been able to sleep more than two or three hours at a time. Although everyone had tried to make sense of it all and move on with life, I could not. I was a complete and total mess. I was trying to trust God and develop a more intimate and personal relationship with Him while at the same time dismiss the negative emotions exhausting my mind. As I finally began to fall asleep, my cell phone rang. On the other end of the line was a scheduler from the airline, notifying me that I was scheduled to work a flight in less than six hours. As I hung up the phone, I began to feel a rush of anxiety overtake my entire mind and body. I started to feel light headed and sick to my stomach. Dear God, please help me was all I could say.

I could not believe it. It had been less than ninety-six hours and they wanted me to return to work as if nothing had happened. I was simply flabbergasted; how could they possibly think I was ready to step back onto an aircraft after this horrid event? Our entire country had been turned upside down. There was absolutely no way that I was going to get on another plane. As I began to contemplate how to get out of this dilemma of going back to work and fulfill my duties as a trained and certified flight attendant for one of the world's largest airlines, I began to shake my head (at my own self). I once again started to reflect on the things that had taken place throughout my life; all the times I had been fearful and God saw me through it all. I remember my pastor from Dallas, TX would always say, "I am the child of a King."

As I began to smile at the memory, I realized who I was and whose I was. I belonged to a God who was above all others. I was the daughter of a King, who was the King of all kings and the Lord of all lords. I had to remind myself that there is no one greater, wiser, better or more powerful than the God whom I serve. I started to reflect on the goodness of God and not on my situation and how afraid I was of the unknown. I put all faith and hope in God, knowing that my help and assurance comes from Him. I love Him more than anything.

Trusting God in The Midst of It All

I entered the flight room of the Newark International Airport with my bags packed, makeup flawless, and a smile that would brighten any passenger's day; anybody in their right mind could see that I was ready. Well, yes, on the outside I was ready and pumped, but on the inside I was broken and terrified. Every negative emotion you can think of was present within me. As I approached the aircraft and met with the rest of my crew, they were all having the same feelings as I was. Checking the aircraft and ensuring the pilots had everything they needed, I thought to myself, *I can do this* (quoting my scripture: Philippians 4:13, *I can do all things through Christ*). You could see the timid and apprehensive looks on everyone's faces. As I made my way down the aisle to the aft of the aircraft, I could feel the tears began to flood my eyes. I immediately ran into the lavatory to grab some tissue. As I looked in to the mirror, I began to sob. I asked "God, why me?" I remembered a song by Fred Hammond, *No Weapon*; I began to sing, "No weapon formed against me shall prosper, it won't work." As I sang the words to this song, I could feel the presence of God in the lavatory with me. My tears began to dry up. My heart began to slow down and I felt the anxiety start to dissipate from my body. I threw up my hands and allowed God to fill me with His peace.

And the peace of God, which surpasses all understanding, will guard your hearts and minds through Christ Jesus. Philippians 4:7

I didn't have to understand the situation; I just needed to know that God was right there with me and that He was in control. Today, my relationship with Him is stronger than it has ever been. I love Him with everything within me.

Although we may face difficulties in our lives and are sometimes fearful of the unknown, know that God is with you. Not only is God with you, but He is within you and He is for you. Romans 8:31 states, *What then shall we say to these things? If God is for us, who can be against us?* Some will continue to live a life consumed by fear, and others will choose a life consumed by the joy of the Lord. God can deliver you from this thing we call fear. He did it for me and I know for a fact He can do it for you too. Establish a personal and intimate relationship with God. Trust and believe in His word and He will keep you in perfect peace. Blessings to each of you.

"Not only is God with you, but He is within you and He is for you."

And one called out to another and said, "Holy, Holy, Holy, is the LORD of hosts, The whole earth is full of His glory."
Isaiah 6:3

LaTasha C. White

LaTasha White is a wife, mother, registered nurse, and a certified John Maxwell leadership coach, speaker, and trainer. She has a strong gift and foundation of faith. Her footsteps are ordered by the Lord, and she has grown to understand she is to wait for his direction before taking a step.

LaTasha has been married to Reginald for 20 years; they are the proud parents of high school freshman, Omar; college freshman, Zharquan, and a 22-year-old young lady, Kiara. LaTasha is the glamma of their 1st grandbaby, two-year old Kamari.

A registered nurse, she has an innate passion for caring for Gods' people, and considers it an honor. This passion shows up in various ways in her life, most recently taking the leap to become a certified coach through the John Maxwell Team and human behavior consultant through Authentic Identity. Early 2016, she and her husband launched Grow Into Victory Intentionally, LLC. At GIVIN, they help individuals blossom into the best version of themselves through mastermind groups, coaching, personality assessments specializing in DISC, and spiritual gift analysis.

LaTasha's heart beat is for the ministry of wives to be the Light in their homes first, then, everywhere else she goes !

CHAPTER FIVE

What's Behind Her Smile?

The Beginning of Us

I was 18 years old with the world at my fingertips, just beginning my adult life and I'd met my prince charming. He swept me off my feet, showered me with gifts, went above and beyond for me, making me feel like I was the only girl in the world. At first, I fell, I fell hard; I had never been treated like this before. Is this what love is supposed to feel like? Is he setting me up? What does he want from me? After all, I'm just a girl from a small town, just 40 miles west of his. Maybe he just wants a girl from a different town because she won't have a way of knowing his true history? These are all questions in my mind, was there any truth to them?

It's a cold, November night, Thanksgiving1995 when our eyes locked for the first time. We were at a party in his hometown. When it was time to leave, we didn't want to leave each other's presence just yet. We went on to a little diner not far down the road, where we chatted for another couple of hours. At about 5am, I realized how late it was. I shrieked, "I have to go, I have to work this morning!"

He wouldn't let me leave without giving him my phone number. I obliged. I jumped in my car, probably breaking all speed limit laws, hurried into my apartment door with a plan to take a quick shower, and prepare for work in record speed. My phone rang as soon as I got in the door. "Who on earth is calling me this time of morning?" I hesitantly answered the phone. It could be Dad, who I shared the apartment with because he wasn't home when I got in. Well, it's not Dad, it's him the guy who I had my eyes glued to all night, who's every word I'd hung on!

Me: Hello…

Him: Hi just wanted to make sure you made it home.

Me: Ok, I'm here getting ready for work.

Him: Ok, I'll call you later.

Me: Ok, goodbye.

I continued my rush to get ready for work, as I think, how nice; he called to see that I made it home. Then in a flash, my next thought was, he's not calling later. I don't have his number (no caller ID on my landline), I can't call him. Would I call him? That's not the lady-like thing to do. Forget about him, he's older, he doesn't want you. Go to work.

I should've been exhausted, but at 18 years old you don't need much sleep. I was a giddy and my heart was a little fluttered over him…him who I should forget about because I would probably never hear from him again. About 3:00pm, I walked in the door prepared to take a short nap and visit family later since it was Thanksgiving weekend. I didn't want to sleep it away. I lay down, hoping secretly hoping he'd call. HE DID!

Over the next several days we talked on the phone whenever we weren't working. Our long-distance phone bills were getting quite high, yet neither one of us seemed to mind. We loved talking with each other, learning about who we were, what our pasts were like, what we loved, and what we didn't. It seemed like an eternity before we'd see each other again. In mid-December he came to town to Christmas shop. I met him at the mall. Falling for him all the more because he was searching high and low for a Barney doll he'd promised his daughter. She was a year old, she would not know if he didn't get it for her, but he'd promised it to her, and she would get it no matter what!

By Valentine's Day we were engaged. I had one stipulation; we would remain celibate until our wedding night. This would be my way of being sure he wanted me for me and not what he could get.

Okay, I've got it all figured out now, I have a handle on things.

About 6 weeks later, I had an epiphany. I'm only 18, he's 25, it's not time for me to settle down yet! All of this is moving too fast, I can't process this. He's probably going to break my heart at some point anyway because he still seems too good to be true. I'm not going to stick around to find out. I'm not going to fall into his trap. I'll show him.

I wait for his nightly call, then I tell him, or more or less blindside him. "We need to break up."

He asked "What happened?"

I reply, "Nothing, it's just all moving too fast for me."

He says "Ok, we can slow down."

I say, "No, I have to be done. You need to take this ring back." I'm thinking if we drag this out any further he's going to break my heart, I'm not going to let him do that. I must make a clean break. I never gave two thoughts to the fact that my actions would break his heart!

He continued to call even after my demands for him not to. Only two weeks had gone by when I decided to take his call one last time. This would be the call that changed the course of our whole life. I agreed to go to a concert with him.

When the tough times get tougher, try to sit in their seat, put your feet in their shoes.

Somehow we resumed right where'd we'd left off, only now without a ring. That's better for me, I told myself, this makes it less committal and scary. By July we decided that we'd proceed with the wedding plans. There was nothing big that changed, nothing that made it less scary for me. I just settled into him, as he made it a point to be attentive. I still needed to prove to myself that he wanted me for me and not what he could get, so we rented our first house together, keeping the celibacy rules in place. We passed the figurative three month move-in trial. October 25, 1996, we wed.

You're probably wiping your brow, thinking finally! Well now the plot thickens. We're married, but do I know how to be a wife? I was fortunate enough to have a great example of what God's plan for marriage looked like right across the street, Mr. and Mrs. Mallory. I was working part time for them and I could see the honor and respect between the two of them. When you're young you don't pay as much attention as you should to what's right in front of you. Without my knowledge, the seed had been planted.

Ok, so we were married. For a couple of years, life was very ordinary; we worked, came home, and spent weekends with friends and family. We were not including God in our week, definitely not our day. Sundays were for resting to us. None of this was super intentional; life was just kind of happening.

The Test of Us

Fast-forward three years, our first son is born, my dad unexpectedly passed away. By the time I thought I was finally somewhat coming to grips with that we would take another blow. At this point, we're still a young married couple of only five to six years, I was in nursing school, and my husband was working a great job that supported us. Everything seemed to be going as planned. You know that kind of calm that causes you to brace yourself for the next blow? God would get my attention.

So here it comes, all of a sudden my husband became very ill. He starts retaining lots of fluid in his legs, all the while no appetite and losing weight at an alarming rate. He slept any hours he wasn't working. We knew this wasn't normal. He was very hesitant to go to the doctor until he couldn't stand the back and abdominal pain any longer. After what would turn out to be many months of testing, surgeries, procedures, and hospitalizations, there were still no answers, and his condition was only worsening. The unproven hypotheses just landed us with mountains of medical bills and not much direction. Finally, at the medical university we would get a diagnosis in 2003. Retroperitoneal Fibrosis... Ok! We've got a diagnosis; what's the treatment? "Well Mr. and Mrs. White, this is where it gets complicated...All we can do is treat the symptoms as they arise, there is no cure."

My heart sank; I felt a pit growing in my stomach. My husband has no questions, no comments, only a blank stare as I pleaded frantically for answers from the team of doctors standing before him. Concerns filled my mind about what the future would bring; he certainly couldn't continue in the state he was in.

There would be more surgeries to protect vital organs from this disease process that threatened to crush anything in its path as it grows in the lower back, wraps around the sides, and finally up the front of his body, blanketing everything in a thick white web that cannot be surgically removed.

We had no way of knowing what the future would hold, especially as the doctors continued to scratch their heads about all of this. He was a completely healthy, 30-year-old man prior to these symptoms surfacing. They have no idea what caused any of this. You mean to tell me there's nothing we can do?

I had joined church a year prior and I was beginning to build my relationship with God. So what I know to do is pray. We know prayer changes things.

We don't have any idea what will come of any of this. Through all of this, our prayer life grew stronger and stronger. My husband joined church with me later. There was nothing else we had to lean on. Along the way, we were blessed with another baby boy. Wow! This was an unexpected blessing; he was God's answer to our cries to show us He was with us.

Want the secret? I worked on myself.

We continued on with doctor appointments, test after test to see if there was anything that could be done. March 2007 my husband was given the news that the disease process, along with all of the testing, had taken its toll on his kidneys, and he'd need to start hemodialysis. All the while, I had a sense of urgency to keep pushing to obtain my nursing degree, I never stopped. Everything in me wanted to give up and concentrate on our family, at the same time I knew I had to push.

May 2007, I graduated and passed state licensing boards as a registered nurse. For us, this was God's grace for me to be able to financially support our family, as my husband would get acclimated to dialysis as the new normal. By the next year, we'd decided to transition his hemodialysis treatments to our home. Praising God all the more that I could do his treatments for him at home, on our schedule, allow him to return to work, and regain some sense of normalcy in our lives.

Every single day, I watch him and the tenacity he has for life and making the most of it. He's made it a point to be an awesome father to our kids, and always putting others ahead of himself even though his condition causes an extreme amount of fatigue and intermittent pain. He always strives to be the best dad he can, and part of that was showing our kids you never give up or give in. He pushed his way through obtaining his first college degree at the age of 42. Our faith in God and his plans for us grow daily despite it all, we know his plan is always perfect.

Now, do not get me wrong, we definitely had our fair share of times throughout the years that made us question it all. We knew better than to ask God *why him*? But, we did ask what does this all mean? What is the lesson in it? We wanted to hurry up and get it so he could get all better then move on with life. That question has gone unanswered even to this day. After two failed kidney transplant evaluations, what we have come to learn is that your tests/life's lessons aren't always for you. Those tests could be for others to see God through you, and begin to learn for themselves how you can always push when you put God first. It is a choice; it is a decision.

They say opposites attract. This is what that looks like for us. I am the ultimate optimist and always see the glass half full. Since I was a little girl, I have often been accused of wearing rose colored glasses by my family. My husband doesn't innately share this same optimism. This is where it became imperative for me to grow my faith so that I could have enough to keep both of us encouraged. I had to stand on God's Word; 1st Corinthians 7:14, *For the unbelieving husband is sanctified by the wife, and the unbelieving wife is sanctified by the husband: else were your children unclean; but now are they holy.*

You can only imagine how tense things got as we all were adjusting. But for my husband, this was his life, his body, his inability to control how good or bad he felt on a given day. I cannot change that, he cannot change that. We have to make the best of this life that we've been blessed to live.

This Is Us

Today, 20 years into our marriage, I reflect on our journey. This is the guy who I ran from. This is the guy I thought was going to use me and break my heart. Yet, this is the guy who I get to share life with. Our three children and our grandson could not have had a better example of never giving in. God's plan in all of this is to show others what the vows "for sickness and in health" really means. If an incurable diagnosis comes, what do you do? We all know what we say we'll do, but do we really know until it is reality? I have learned so much through our trials and grown more than I can explain here.

The biggest thing I did learn is how to be a wife! Want the secret? I worked on myself. Not rocket science, but definitely not something I was doing. During our early years I became unlikable, verging on unlovable. I'd let the stress get the best of me at times. It's easy to become frustrated and snap back when we're anxious about things that are going on that we can't control. What I came to know, and have to work to keep at the forefront of my mind daily, is I cannot change the state of anything or anyone, only myself. The way I respond and the way I react are my responsibility.

Over the years so many people have asked about how we deal with everything. What we know to be true is that if we take care of God's business, he will take care of ours. For example; we wanted to take our children on vacation like everyone else. How could we do this? We have the dialysis machine and supplies at home, how would we get it to another state? Granted, it's not as easy for us to get away as other people. Thankfully, my brother has been generous enough to allow us to borrow his truck, year after year, to load all the medical supplies in the back so we could take summer vacations. We decided we plan the treatments around the vacation activities. Is it easy? Of course not! Is it worth the memories for our family? 1,000%!

We are absolutely no good to anyone if we lie down and let life roll us over. Most things in life require work, whether it's pushing through an illness, pushing through a job that you don't love, pushing through raising children well, or even pushing through a workout. The common denominator is we must push. There truly is a way when there is a will.

Tough Love Wisdom for Wives

It's so easy to give in to circumstances when we don't think there's anything we can do about it. I once heard, life is 10% what happens to us, and 90% how we respond to what happened. If you chew on that, process it, and keep it in your awareness, you can change your life.

God's got us no matter what, and knowing I could tell him about my heartache, my dreams, my desires, my frustrations, and my inadequacies, changed my entire world. If you notice, everything I spoke about is ME. That's the only person I could change.

When our husbands hurt, we hurt. It's hard to sit by and watch them deal with the pressures of learning a new normal, that could include anything from the inability to work and provide to feeling physically and emotionally subpar. Our faith changed our outlook on *everything*. Our role, as wives, is to support them. It was something I had to grow through. When the tough times get tougher; try to sit in their seat, put your feet in their shoes. Do not take things personally. Love him through it. Let him feel safe to vent his frustrations. Always lift him up. Let him feel what he feels. Be that positive wind behind him.

This is our glimpse of glory. I am honored to be Mrs. Reginald L. White. I am honored that God chose me for him. We choose to 'see God in the midst of it all' and persist through our pain to our purpose. Our prayer is that this has blessed someone who feels that picking their head up off the pillow is next to impossible, for someone who is a wife and has no idea how to support her husband, for someone who has to believe for their spouse when they can't believe for themselves, for someone who needs a reminder that life is really not as bad as it seemed. Rise up, this world needs you!

Endnotes:
Corinthians 7:14 KJV

Jannifer Denise

Jannifer Denise desires to encourage, empower and educate in the areas of wellness and self-care. She is a wellness coach, child advocate, public speaker, and self-care product artisan. Founding the lifestyle brand, LoveLifeWell LLC in 2014, Jannifer has a genuine passion for health and wellness. Jannifer discovered how important the element of self-care is to optimum wellness and became a strong advocate for proper self-care. Her efforts to encourage, empower, and educate has enabled her to serve in a variety of capacities as a mentor, teacher, advocate, and coach in the city of Indianapolis, IN.

Working with a variety of local organizations in addition to her own, Jannifer hopes to continue to bring to light the importance of self-care as an addition to wellness in her community. Jannifer has been a featured guest speaking on the importance of wellness and self-care on shows such as *Medically Speaking*, a health focused radio talk show on the local Radio One affiliate, as well as other talk shows in her city. In addition to mentor, teacher, and advocate, Jannifer has served with non-profit and public organizations to stand in the gaps for children in her community.

Giving her efforts and energy to causes she truly believes in, Jannifer genuinely strives to serve her community in a grand way.

CHAPTER SIX

Finding Glory

Every Story Has a Beginning

As I screamed, pleaded, and banged my fists against the icy walls of the dark deep freezer I truly believed I would never get out. My petite ten-year-old frame clothed only in shorts and a tank top began to shiver from fear and the frost forming on my skin. I yelled in anger and fear as I heard them laugh and discuss how long they would remain on top of the deep freezer trapping me inside. My screams of anger and frustration eventually turned to pleadings of mercy trying to explain that I no longer wanted to play. I explained how I promised not to tell anyone if they would only let me go. I bargained the only resources I knew I possessed: candy and doing their chores for months to come if they would release me from my imprisonment. What seemed like moments of fun and games to my siblings felt like an eternity to me. I don't recall how long I remained in that freezing dark space lying on top of frozen groceries, however for a child already suffering from a sense of not belonging or fitting in with my family this was yet again an experience that reaffirmed my feelings of detachment where I should have experienced inclusion within my Home.

They released me and exhaustively tried to assure me that it was only a game in hopes I would not tell our parents when they returned. However, the ringing thoughts of disconnect and isolation would remain in my mind for years to come. As a child, I could not understand why I did not experience the feelings of belonging among family, nor why I was regularly persuaded to believe that all my family residing outside of my household were such terrible people. Feelings of distrust and disconnect would continue to be a major factor in my childhood. Those closest to me seemed at the time to cause more pain and feelings of disconnect than those I occasionally had the pleasure of existing among. I would later learn that God used my isolation to strengthen my relationship with Him.

Breaking and Building

While my intention is to leave a positive mark on the world, I have discovered that life will not always be free from trial, hurt, and frustration. Test and trial are not only necessary, they are inevitable. It is how we overcome what we experience that allows us to stand in the gaps for others and to truly show the power of God. The very things we experience that seem like they were designed to destroy us are the painful fires that God allows to develop us like crucibles of rare gold.

To build strong muscles in the human body the muscle must first be broken down. This developing process can be hard and seem unbearable. The breaking process is, however, necessary for the growth process. With the developing experience in our lives we can feel broken, alone, and singled out. Many times, we don't realize how God can truly get the glory amid our pain until later in our stories. The test is for us to hold out and keep faith that God will use us just as we are; broken, hurt, stained, and cause us to become whole, healed, and forgiven.

A longing for connection was such a strange thing to experience in my home that consisted of siblings and both of my parents. If I did not belong there in my home, where did I belong? Was it school perhaps? Maybe amongst neighborhood friends? I had not reached a state of maturity vast enough to think of asking God where I belonged. Instead, I intentionally chose to seek connection elsewhere: friends, Sunday school teachers, and school teachers alike. I found most of my connections would later be with those much older than myself. If I did not belong in my home, surely I belonged outside with others in my community. However, I would later decide to wear the cloak of solitude instead to hide scars that might prevent me from belonging among those outside my home as well.

A Costly Ride

I tried to convince him to release his grip on my shoulders as he pinned me down on a bed in a dark cluttered room. While he undressed me I remember thinking to try not to anger him for fear that if I did I may never be able to leave. Fear paralyzed my body and caused my voice to shake as I tried to politely convince him not to force himself on me. Fear would not allow me to fight back more than telling him I had not done this before and did not want to do it now. At

The very things we experience that seem like they were designed to destroy us are the painful fires that God allows to develop us like crucibles of rare gold.

the tender age of thirteen I had accepted that the grown man forcing himself on me was my fault and that I could not go Home and tell anyone because I was in the wrong for going along with a friend to a house I had not been given permission to visit. I had been trying to fit in. I didn't want to seem un-cool so I agreed to climb into the front seat of the freshly washed luxury sedan and go along for a ride with a friend and the man she assured me was a good guy for what was promised to be just a short trip and back.

As I lay under him I realized I had no control except to not overreact so that I could get out of there alive. As a last attempt to be released I mustered the strength to yell for my friend in the other room. When I was finally released from under his grip, I grabbed as much of my clothes as I could find in the dark and ran to dress in the hallway. All I could think of was getting out of that house. I had clearly failed at fitting in once again and promised myself if I made it out that I would

70

never try to fit in again. At the naïve age of thirteen I did not know what this experience meant for me, however I knew I could not tell anyone, not even my friend who later asked when I entered the living room why I had yelled for her from behind the closed door. I knew I was not yet safe still standing in that house so I joked that he was just being silly. Once Home I decided not to mention the terrifying adult situation I experienced. I had made it out of that house, which had become my goal that evening, so there was no reason to have experienced the punishment from life for going along where I did not belong and subject myself to the punishment from Home I believed I would receive instead of the support I needed.

From that night on I regularly had night terrors where I had no control in varying situations. As I lay in my twin sized bed in a room still filled with dolls and stuffed animals, I desperately tried to forget what I had experienced. I told no one and eventually blocked out the event entirely until years later. While I had many of the same night terrors night after night I grew to forget why and when they began and accepted that I simply had an issue and fear of loss of control.

I found myself always on guard. I became very judgmental and untrusting of people. I knew that I loved and enjoyed being around people, however I was regularly told at Home how bad people were. I had already experienced for myself the pain of trying to belong. I lacked a sense of belonging to any group or sect of people so it would be best for me to not completely trust anyone. I had learned early on that Home was not the safe space I needed to exist in my flaws, and outside was no different.

Healing from Home

Years later I stood outside my college dorm in the chilling January temperatures with my jacket unzipped and my eyes closed, my heart raced as warm salty tears ran down my face. I finally found a place I could breathe, outside in the freezing cold wind. I was now discovering that anxiety attacks would be added to the list of terrifying experiences. Unlike some of the other experiences for me, I would experience panic and anxiety attacks over and over. Triggered by the most random things, anxiety attacks would cause me to withdraw further from family and friends to do what I had learned early on to do, deal with it on my own.

To literally suffocate in open air would be my new terror. The regular need to exit the building or open a window in freezing temperatures just to breathe would soon overtake my life. I could not sit in class without breaking down and crying. As time went on hyperventilation from anxiety interfered with my ability to enjoy simple activities like driving from one location to the next without having to pull over to cry and catch my breath. What was wrong with me? No one else seemed to be overwhelmed by the random thoughts of forgetting to turn the light switch off weeks prior, or making the wrong turn on the highway the day before. The very things that would plague my mind and cripple me at random were things of little or no significance at all, yet I felt guilty and overwhelmed by the thoughts.

While Home had not previously been a safe space for me growing up it would soon bless me with the introduction of positive affirmations. When I typically thought of Home I ruminated feelings of hurt, disconnect, mental illness, being dropped off at the guardian home, or put out as a teenager and other events that did not seem conducive to my wellbeing. However, one day I had no one else to call except Home. As I cried and gasped frantically trying to explain what I was experiencing the voice on the other end of the line instructed me to boldly tell my anxiety, "You serve me no good purpose!" This sounded like hocus pocus. To literally speak to my anxiety. To say out loud, "You serve me no good purpose," would seem odd to do, however it would prove to be literally life-saving. I was then told to remember 2 Timothy 1:7, *For God hath not given us the spirit of fear, but of power and of love and a sound mind.*

Was I healing from a place that had long plagued my life with hurt? While Home had not always been a safe space for me it was where I was introduced to Christ at a young age. It was my belief in and relationship with God that sustained me throughout my years of complacency. It would now be that same connection to God that would create a space for healing and deliverance.

Later during a conversation at Home I was asked when I believed my anxiety began and what I felt was causing it. As I thought over the recent experiences in my life, I began to share how I had learned early on to hide the things that seemed to stain who I was told I was supposed to be. I shared how I learned that I did not have safe space to be flawed, so I buried anything that appeared to have wrinkle or stain. I explained my recent abortion no one knew about might have been the tipping block to being overwhelmed with everything I hid away. I recounted experiences from my childhood where I did not feel I had safe space to exist. Among the experiences I recounted was that terrifying occurrence of sexual assault that had remained untold.

While it pained Home to hear that I had not believed it was a safe space to tell of my sexual assault when it happened almost ten years prior, I also realized that burying such serious experiences was what had caused me to become full of anxiety in the first place. Compacting my feelings of fear, hurt, and shame had given me a sense of control over circumstances I experienced when I felt I had little or no control. I believed that burying those feelings meant it didn't happen or I would not be victimized by the experiences. Unfortunately, the buildup of things buried had begun to take a toll on my life.

Now I was all exposed. Things I had become protective over for so many years were now out in the open. I had held onto secrets and hurt for so many years. The time had now come to let go. However long and uncomfortable the process of healing from past hurts would be, I knew that it was necessary. God was ever more important in this stage of my life because the initial inclination was to blame and be the victim in what seemed to be a tumultuous story. Being the victim, however, would not serve any purpose. I could not grow from experiences I remained bound to. I would have to learn to be ever more reliant on God for strength in the process of letting go.

Finding Forgiveness

God gave the ultimate sacrifice of his son Jesus Christ in forgiveness of our sins. If God can forgive us of our faults, who are we to... who am I not to forgive others that may have wronged me through intentional or circumstantial acts? Who am I not to forgive myself? Did forgiveness mean dismissing the hurt and pain? Of course not, however it did mean releasing the power previous incidents had over me. Forgiveness is more about freeing one's self of bondage than it is about acquitting others of their wrong doing. I learned that I did not have to be confined or controlled by my experiences. I no longer had to carry the very things I wished to be so far removed from. It was now up to me to spend time with God to understand His purpose and direction for my life.

I no longer had to carry the very things I wished to be so far removed from.

But we also rejoice in our sufferings because we know that suffering produces perseverance; perseverance, character; and character, hope. Romans 5:3-4.

I would later hear someone explain that purging the past does not mean forgetting, it means releasing. I began the process of releasing in hopes to become who God truly desired me to be.

We often conceal and hide our pain, as I did, to prevent others from seeing how flawed we are. One problem with hiding hurt is that you are not positioned to be healed properly. The other problem with hiding hurt is that others are not able to see the work God has done in your life. You rob God of a testimony when you don't allow others to see what He has brought you through. It is important to embrace our pasts, imperfections, and short comings to showcase the power of God in our lives today. If God can move in our lives He can move in the lives of those around us.

In the process of forgiving I learned that I was never alone. God had kept and preserved me throughout my experiences. I realized how blessed I had been in spite of my circumstances. Years later I would learn that people don't do things *to you*, rather they do things *for themselves*. It has been said another way that *hurt people, hurt people*. I began to feel compassion for those who had been so hurt as to inflict pain on me. What had they experienced that caused them not to live and act in love? I selfishly felt better knowing that there was not something wrong with me that caused me to be subjected to such pain. Finding God in life's toughest situations is how we know our experiences were not meant to break us, rather to build us.

For I know the plans I have for you, declares the LORD, plans to prosper you and not to harm you, plans to give you hope and a future. Jeremiah 29:11.

There was also great healing in discovering I was not alone in unfortunate experiences. To meet others who had triumphed despite their own circumstances was life affirming. Through the transparency of others, I began to see how what I had experienced positioned me to better serve, advocate for, and love on those around me. I began to see my circumstances as groundwork for allowing me to be an instrument of the very things I once longed for; acceptance, advocacy, and love. I prize my relationship with God, while imperfect, that has remained the guiding force for my life. As a result, I began to fall in love with the woman God was creating me to be.

Affirming God's Glory

Positive affirmations remain instrumental for me in overcoming feelings of fear, anxiety, self-doubt, and circumstantial heaviness. Like the declaration I had been instructed to speak over my anxiety some time ago, I learned that I had command over my emotions and life. Experiences would not have more power over my life than I had. Affirmations are audible daily reminders of who God created me to be regardless of what I may experience. Affirmations are also commands for things to come.

One of my favorite set of morning affirmations are:

I am amazing.
I am forgiven.
I am abundantly blessed.
The universe conspires to bless me.
I can do ALL things through Christ that gives me strength.
The Lord is my Shepherd, I shall not want.

Those few lines and a moment of prayer and meditation are my daily conditioning to face whatever life throws at me. I encourage the beautiful soul reading this to find three to five lines that speak life into your own soul as well. I encourage you to invest time in your healing and self-care. Self-care is essential. Lastly, I invoke you to see purpose in your pain. God can use what He allowed you to experience to be the platform for your service to others.

It is through our transparency that we showcase the work God has done in our lives. Matthew 5:16 says, *Let your light shine before men, that they may see your good deeds and praise your Father in heaven.*

Ericka Bond

Ericka C. Bond's desire is to see young girls nurtured, informed, and empowered so they can boldly be who they were created to be. Ericka is a native of Jackson, TN and currently resides in Radcliff, KY. She is the eldest of two children and the proud aunt of four nephews and one niece. An active member of Restoration Worship Center, she proudly serves as one of the leaders of the Women's Ministry Team and as a member of the Worship Team. She created a mentoring program for girls, Y-LOVE, Inc., (Young Ladies of Virtue and Excellence). Y-LOVE, Inc is facilitated in the school system reaching over 150 girls. The girls meet once a month and participate in learning life skills and other activities that empower them.

Ericka received her bachelors of arts degree with/entrepreneurship from Ashford University. Because of her passion for creating beautiful things and her love for sports, she started her event planning company EPIC Events, LLC (Ericka Presents Incredible Creations). She will attend Georgetown University this spring in pursuit of her master's degree in sports industry management/concentration in sports entertainment.

Ericka believes that we all have been destined for greatness and we all have different paths for us as individuals. One of her favorite quotes is "Purpose is the reason you journey. Passion is the fire that lights your way." Author Unknown.

CHAPTER SEVEN

Hey! I Am Good

The Lie Depression Loves to Tell

*L**ife is made up of a collection of moments that are not ours to keep. The pain we encounter throughout our days spent on this earth comes from the illusion that some moments can be held onto. Clinging to people and experiences that were never ours in the first place is what causes us to miss out on the beauty of the miracle that is the now. All of this is yours, yet none of it is. How could it be? Look around you. Everything is fleeting, Rachel Brathen*

Acknowledgement is a Key to Change

For years, I could not bring myself to one, acknowledge the fact that I was depressed, and two, I could not verbalize it. I was literally imprisoned by this illness. I felt hopeless and concluded this would be my life for the rest of my life. My life consisted of moments that were not mine to keep. Yet there was something in me that caused me to hold on to every moment of my life whether good or bad. They were my moments and I could not understand why I had to release what was mine. What I could not grasp was the fact that the moments were sent to propel me to my next phase of life. Since I could not comprehend that the very thing I was holding on to was supposed to be my teaching moment, I failed over and over, repeating the same test time after time because I refused to learn the lessons. I may have been in a different location and the characters may have been different, but the essence of the lessons were the same. When I did not learn or even acknowledge there were lessons to be learned, in addition to my disobedience, thrust me into the dark world of depression for many years.

Per *Mental Health of America* every year more than 19 million Americans suffer from some type of depressive illness. Mayo Clinic defines depression as a mood disorder that causes a persistent feeling of sadness and loss of interest. Clinical depression affects how you feel, think, and behave. It can lead to a variety of emotional and physical problems. It may cause trouble doing normal day-to-day activities, and sometimes you feel as if life isn't worth living.

While battling depression, I was in constant physical pain. There were times when I literally thought I was having a heart attack because I was in endless pain from my neck down to my arm on my left side. I did not realize the toll depression was taking on my body. I did not relate my aches and pains to depression until I began to do the research. The symptoms or signs may vary from person to person, but some of the common symptoms are but are not limited to; feelings of sadness, tearfulness, emptiness or hopelessness, angry outbursts, irritability, or frustration, sleep disturbances, and feelings of worthlessness.

There was a point in my journey that I was going to the doctor so much because I was having all types of physical ailments, or so I thought. After many visits my doctor asked me if she could have a conversation with me, not as my doctor, but as my friend. She told me that I was not physically ill but depressed. She had run every test known to man but could not find anything physically wrong with me. As she explained to me why she felt I was depressed I listened to what she had to say. She was a Caucasian lady and I told her, "Black people don't get depressed." There was no way I could be depressed.

For years, I was in denial, refusing to believe I was battling depression. I learned how to live with the illness while pretending to have it all together. My normal became smiling on the outside, appearing to have it all together, but crumbling on the inside. My favorite cover-up line was "I am good." No matter how sad I was, how mentally tormented I was, how many times I wanted to retreat and be alone I would always say, "I am good." I learned how to function. My cover-up was so good my cousin told me she had no clue until I shared at church what I had been going through, even though we had been living together.

Fifteen years after the initial conversation with my doctor I was finally able to acknowledge and admit

I was battling depression. I was having one of my weeks. I was in a perpetual state of sadness when I cried out to God. I was sick and tired of being sick and tired. I asked God, "What is wrong with me?"

It is normal to be sad when life hands you some unfortunate situations and circumstances however, what is not normal is to go day-in and day-out sad and weighed down. I waited for God to answer. He told me, "You are battling depression."

Like the conversation I had fifteen years' prior with my doctor, I had it with God.

"No, God I am not depressed I am just weighed down with life." As I sat in silence replaying what God had spoken to me, it hit me like a ton of bricks…I AM DEPRESSED. That was a hard pill to swallow, but it was one I had to ingest. I cried and I asked God, "How did I get here?"

As always, I asked and He answered. He took me back to another time fifteen years ago, when a group of us would pray together seeking God for our next move. During prayer God would show me where He wanted to take me. When prayer was over and even though I had asked God to show me where He was taking me, my response was, "I am not doing that. I am not that person and I am not qualified for that."

A Mind is a Terrible Thing to Waste-UNCF

Instead of me trusting that He had equipped me to do what He showed me I decided I was not qualified and discounted myself. The problem with that is I opened myself up to years of unnecessary heartache and pain because I did not trust the plan God had for my life. God is so full of love and mercy that as I began to seek Him regarding how to slay this giant He began to bring scriptures to mind. Through the process, I had to make sure that I prayed, fasted, studied the scriptures, and praised God daily. These were essentials for my deliverance. I could not do one and omit the other and get the deliverance and freedom I so desired.

Another aspect of my deliverance and freedom was changing my thought life. Proverbs 23:7 KJV says *As a man thinketh in his heart so is he.* This is so key for me to stay free. I must think intentionally.

Dr. Patrick Gentempo says it best "What you thought before has led to every choice you have made, and this adds up to you at this moment. If you want to change who you are physically, mentally, and spiritually, you will have to change what you think."

Our thoughts create our worlds. I had to admit my life was not the life I wanted because of my toxic thinking. My thoughts created the life I was living. I had to take ownership for the life that I was living and decide I could continue life as I knew it or I could create the life I wanted through my thought life along with prayer, God's Word, and faith. Philippians 4:8 KJV says, *Finally, brethren, whatsoever things are true, whatsoever things are honest, whatsoever things are just, whatsoever things are pure, whatsoever things are lovely, whatsoever things are of good report; if there be any virtue, and if there be any praise, think on these things.*

This is where intentional thinking comes in. I am still learning when the negative thoughts and negative self-talk tries to rear its ugly head I must offset the negative thought with a positive. It is not always easy, but when you get sick and tired of the sadness, being weighed down, or your life not looking the way you want it to look you will dig deep and fight those thoughts with everything you have in you.

2 Corinthians 10:5 KJV provides us with instructions on how to counteract the negative self-talk and thoughts. *Casting down imaginations, and every high thing that exalts itself against the knowledge of God, and bringing into captivity every thought to the obedience of Christ.* This scripture is specific when dealing with thoughts that are contradictory to the Word. It tells us to take the thought captive. You may wonder, "How do I do that?" The Word of God is a great place to start. For every negative thought the enemy brings to us there is a scripture that can disarm and dismantle it.

You Cannot Have a Positive Life and a Negative Mind, Joyce Meyer

To know the promises of God when the enemy attacks us in our minds takes time of studying the Word of God. You can't win the war if you have not prepared for battle. You must be armed and ready for battle; you can't be getting ready when the enemy attacks you.

Trying to prepare for battle while fighting the battle is a sure way to guarantee your defeat. I have tried so many times to simultaneously fight and prepare for battle and guess what? Defeat was my portion. It didn't have to be, but I chose to fail by not preparing for battle. The enemy is after our minds; the word tells us in Romans 7:25 AMP, *Thanks, be to God (for my deliverance) through Jesus Christ our Lord!*

So then, on the one hand I, with my mind, serve the laws of God but on the other, with my flesh (my human nature, my worldliness, my sinful capacity) I serve the law of sin. It is with our minds that we serve the Lord. This scripture brought so much light, so much revelation to me. It caused me to have a clearer understanding of why the enemy's goal was to keep my mind in mayhem. If my mind is in constant turmoil I cannot serve the Lord properly. When my mind was in ceaseless chaos I often envisioned my mind being like a catastrophic war zone; debris and rubble everywhere while I tried to figure out how to rebuild after the tragedy.

There is no set formula or guidelines for getting your life back. Each person's process is different, so what works for me may not be what will work for you. What I do know is if you ask God to show you the process you need to take He will do it. I asked God to continue showing me anything that contributed to the depressed state that I was in. He revealed I was comparing myself to others. I shared this with a friend and she gave me a scripture which talks about how foolish it is to compare ourselves to others. We have the audacity to put ourselves in the same class or compare ourselves with some who (supply testimonials to) commend themselves. When they measure themselves by themselves and compare themselves, they lack wisdom and behave as fools, 2 Corinthians 10:12 AMP. It is tragic when we compare ourselves to others. God has given all of us our own paths and He predestined our appointed times for victories and manifestations. We often look at others walking in their victories and compare it to where we are on our journey. What we fail to realize is we don't know the back story to their victory.

I am learning that I need to stay in my lane and be grateful to God for my journey that will manifest the breakthroughs, victories, and deliverance I so desire. At one point, I was so miserable I felt if I could just find me another job I would feel better. I was actively seeking at every turn. I was on Indeed, Monster, CareerBuilder, and reaching out to any and every one I thought could assist me with getting a better job. One day in my frustration I was talking to God about how I was feeling. I told him I didn't understand what He was doing in my life and I just didn't understand why He has not blessed me with a better job, etc. He told me I hadn't asked what his plan was for my life. He brought Jeremiah 29:11 KJV to mind where He knows the plans and thoughts toward us. He shared with me that I had not asked him what the plan was. He told me that I didn't have to ask for anything nor was there anything else He must do because the plan for my life was already laid out. All I had to do was thank him for showing me the doors He would open or the people I needed in my life that would assist with me going to the next level. The plan is already set; your victory is predestined, all you have to do is thank God that He will reveal the plan He has for your life.

As Iron Sharpens Iron, so does a Friend Sharpen a Friend-King Solomon

God has people in place to assist you with your deliverance and freedom. Be open because sometimes He uses people you not ever expect. Just as God has people to assist with your victory be careful not to open yourself up to those the enemy send that are a part of his plan for your demise. You need people in your life that not only speak to where you are, but those that speak to and call forth the man or woman of God you were predestined to be. Amos 3:3 NLT says, *Can two people walk together without agreeing on the direction?* Ask God to remove all of those that don't add to your life. If you have people in your life that speak contradictory to what you know God has said about you then it is time to let them go.

True friends will call you out when you are out of line, but it is done in love. Proverbs 27:17 NLT says, *As iron sharpens iron, so a friend sharpens a friend.* We need those people that sometimes rub us the wrong way and its okay if it is done to thrust you into a better situation or to put you in a better mind space. We need each other to grow, but we need the right people in our lives. You need people that you can completely be transparent with and there be absolutely no judgement. What I learned through my journey is once you admit there is a problem to yourself first, then to others, you take away the enemies' power to torment you.

Accountability is so crucial for your success in defeating the giant that has you stuck in any area of your life. Ecclesiastes 4:9 MSG says, *It's better to have a partner than go it alone. Share the work, share the wealth. And if one falls, the other helps.* If you don't already have those friends that are just as passionate about your deliverance and freedom as you are then ask God to send them into your life. Living a life of freedom and peace is hard to walk in at times, but once you have experienced that life you will fight because your life depends on it to ensure you never go back to your old ways of thinking and living.

> *The one thing we know for sure is that God wants us to be free and live a life free of worry, doubt, sadness, and fear*

Galatians 5:1 MSG says *Christ has set us free to live a free life. So, take your stand!* Never again let anyone put a harness of slavery on you. Once God has liberated you do whatever you must do to stay in that place. That could mean cutting off friends or family, being mindful of the conversations you have, the music you listen to, television shows, etc. It could be a multiplicity of things. Even if you are not sure what they are, ask God, He will show you, then be open to whatever God reveals to you.

In the End, We Win

The one thing we know for sure is that God wants us to be free and live a life free of worry, doubt, sadness, and fear. His desire is that we have life and have it more abundantly. Living under the dark cloud of depression is not a life of abundance ordained by God. Any and everything that keeps you from the God ordained life ask him to reveal it. Once He does, ask him to give you a strategy to remove it. Psalms 144:1 lets us know when we are in battle and if we don't know how to defeat our enemy we can ask God to teach our fingers to fight and our hands to war. In other words, if we don't have a strategy for victory all we have to do is ask God and He will teach us how to fight.

I love the quote "Freedom isn't free" by Retired Air Force Colonel Ryan Gremillion. We are in a constant battle to remain free from the attacks that keep us from being who God predestined us to be. I promise, based on my experience, once you have slayed your giant that has held you captive for years you will be willing to fight if you must to remain free and experience the exceeding and abundant life God tells us in Ephesian 3:20 we can have.

Endnotes:

Proverbs 23:7 KJV
2 Corinthians 10:5 KJV
Philippians 4:8 KJV
Romans 7:25 AMP
2 Corinthians 10:12
Jeremiah 29:11 KJV
Amos 3:3 NLT

Psalms 144:1 KJV
Ecclesiastes 4:9 MSG
Proverbs 27:17 NLT
Galatians 5:1 MSG
Ephesians 3:20 KJV

Stephanie Bowie

Stephanie Bowie is a certified life coach, trainer, and owner of Coach Steph B and B Empowered, LLC. Her focus is helping others identify and pursue their passions, and achieving their visions in the areas of career, leadership, and personal finance. Stephanie has developed training solutions and workshops for organizations such as the Federal Women's Program. She has taught business courses at Martin University and the Business Owner's Initiative.

Stephanie earned her bachelor's degree in accounting and finance from IUPUI in 2005, and is completing her MBA at Anderson University. In 1992 she joined the US Army Reserves, and became a financial management specialist in 2003. She is currently a finance instructor and trains hundreds of soldiers per year in the full spectrum of financial operations as well as leadership.

Stephanie is a member of The Way International, which is a "Biblical research, teaching, and fellowship ministry dedicated to presenting the accuracy and practicality of God's Word (www.theway.org)." One of her foundational scriptures is Mark 9:23, *Jesus said unto him, if thou canst believe, all things are possible to him that believeth.* It stands as a reminder and exhortation to believe that we are who God says we are, we have what God says we have, and we can do what God says we can do!

CHAPTER EIGHT

Who Am I?

"The world will ask you who you are, and if you don't know, the world will tell you." Carl Jung

The Interview

Natural sunlight flooded the room from the oversize windows spanning both exterior walls of the sixth floor office. Directly across from the door entry to my right was a small, glass table with three contemporary styled chairs around it. I sat on a green leather loveseat tucked against an interior wall, and adjacent to the large, glass desk just to my right. It was L-shaped, and placed facing the door and table. The room was classy and warm. Advertising manuals with intricate graphics on their covers were stacked neatly on the end table next to the loveseat. Lush green plants made the space feel like home. Everything was beautiful, yet functional. Everything had a place, and a purpose.

Seated behind the table was the president and CEO of the company...immaculately dressed. He had on what had to be the most expensive suit I had ever seen, with a cashmere-type thin sweater underneath the jacket. He was polished, professional, and had a very calm demeanor. It was friendly, and yet not overly excitable. In the words of some old school folks, he was "cool, calm, and collected."

I angled myself on the loveseat to face toward his desk. I was nervous in my brown polyester sheath dress and brown loafer slides. It was the most professional outfit I had at the time, and yet I felt its woeful inadequacy.

We exchanged a couple of pleasantries and I answered a couple of basic questions. And then came the question that would change the course of the interview, and my life, dramatically.

"Do you have any sales experience?" He asked.

The question seemed simple enough. It was a yes or no answer. There has always been something very transparent about me. I thought long and hard through my professional history. Military – NO. Fast food? No. Chinese beauty supply? No. Cleaning lady? No. I thought hard about my job history, and especially about my most recent job…

The Mistaken Identity

"And now, coming to the stage…the cutie with the big ole' booty! Some call her smooth…some call her sexy…but tonight, gentlemen put your hands together fooorrrr…..Jaazzzzyyyyyy!" The DJ boomed over the loud speaker, holding my name until his lungs were almost out of air.

I gulped down the last of my Crown and Coke and darted from the dressing room as my music selection began to play. Right before I emerged into the spotlight, I slowed my pace to a slow and seductive walk. I steadied my breathing, and lowered my eyes to a sultry slant. Caramel brown Crown Royal coursed through my body, warming me and supplying the much needed liquid courage. All eyes were on me as I sashayed my scantily clad body down the walkway. I weaved my way around the small tables in rhythmic motion to the end of the stage. Ever so slowly, I climbed the three steps up.

"Baby – baby – bayyyy...beee," the smooth voices of Dru Hill and Mariah Carey filled the airwaves. I grabbed the pole with my right hand, and circled the stage, slightly dragging my feet clad with shimmery silver six-inch platform heels.

The stage, about three feet high with large round platform areas on each end, connected by a narrow walkway was just big enough for two girls to pass one another. If viewed from above, it might look like an over-sized dumbbell. I let go of the pole, and danced my way down the walkway to the opposite end of the stage.

"What's it gonna be?" the duo sang on, as I reached my destination on the other platform. With one hand I grabbed the slender pole, kicked out powerfully, and wrapped my body backwards around the pole, sending myself into a rapid spin.

Spinning around, I saw my surroundings in 360 degrees. The room was lit with black lights and neon signs hanging from the wall behind the bar. Around the entire perimeter of the stage were small tables that sat three chairs comfortably. On the side of the club opposite the door was a long bar lined with bar stools.

Adjacent to the bar sat the DJ booth, also elevated about three feet off the ground. This was always a hub of activity.

"Ohhh baby baby baaabbbbbyyy..." I finished my spin and noticed a couple of men had moved to be seated at the stage, indicating their desire for a close-up dance, and their willingness to tip me for my services. I dropped to my knees and worked the floor, moving from guest to guest until I had personally entertained each one.

"Is it him, or is it meee?" I continued my show through the end of the song. Then performed for another, faster tune.

I felt a sense of power as I exited the stage and headed toward one of the men who had spent several minutes at the stage. This investment of a little time and money was an indicator that he may want a private dance. This was where the real money was made, in the back room. After a few songs (two for $20), I collected my money, hugged my client, and headed to the dressing room to freshen up and change for the next set. I sat there in that small, makeshift dressing room, face to face with myself in a large dirty mirror chipped around the edges. Looking back at me was someone I didn't really know. An impersonator. A young lady trying desperately to be the part she looked.

I got my introduction to stripping in early 1997 in Nashville, TN. I had just completed my associates of arts degree and had learned that a good friend of mine had moved down to Nashville. I immediately thought about Tennessee State University, and HBCU in that area, and went to visit her. We made plans to get a place together, and I would enroll in TSU that following fall.

My first night there visiting I went with her to her job to hang out. It was my first time ever at a strip club, and it was electric! There was an energetic buzz about the place as half naked women strutted around carrying Crown Royal bags. Drinks flowed freely, as did the money. The ladies were stunning in their confidence. They were laughing, drinking, dancing, and having fun and getting paid to do it.

That night I had a few drinks and sat at the bar talking to whoever was sitting next to me. At times, I would go into the dressing room with my friend and lounge while she and other ladies changed in between sets. It was a very small room with thick black carpet and a couple of chairs. There was one big mirror that sat on the floor and leaned against a wall, which everyone used to do make-up and final checks before heading back out onto the floor.

One night, one of the strippers looked at me and said, "What a shame. You got one of the best bodies in here and don't even dance..."

She struck a nerve. I had already begun to visualize myself doing what they did. Prancing around a club full of men, half naked, drinking and dancing and collecting more money than I had ever seen to that point. The next time that the costume lady came in with a rack full of clothes, I bought my first outfit. Two days later, I was on the stage. My first job as a stripper lasted about three weeks. The plan that my friend and I had agreed to wasn't happening for several reasons beyond our control at that time. So I moved on, and found myself down in Georgia near Ft. Stewart. Once again, I turned to dancing to make money.

Miscalculated Worth

How did I end up here? I mean, this is not a place that you plan to be...you don't exactly talk to your high school counselor about this job. My journey to this stage was predictable, perhaps even ordained. For as long as I could remember, I patterned my life after others. I always felt that other girls knew something that I didn't. They knew who they were. At that time, my friend was a bona fide hustler. She knew who she was, and she lived it out. I wasn't so sure about my place in life.

Who I am is acceptable. I did not have to hide my truth in order to receive what God planned for me!

I had no sense of self-worth, no standard for life, and no direction or plan. In my earliest memories, I felt inadequate in every way. Lacking something at my core. Insufficient. Irrelevant. Not quite enough. I didn't believe that I was anyone special, certainly no one to cherish. I was wandering. Lost. And out of this place of mistaken identity, I made decisions and choices that lined up with Jazzy.

So here I sat in a makeshift dressing room, drinking my fourth Crown and Coke and headed out for my next set on stage...

The Promotion

Back at the interview, I pondered the answer to the question at hand. Did I have any sales experience?

It felt like an eternity had passed by, and I could come up with no valid sale experience at all. In fact, I hated sales. I could only think of one job where sales of any sort were involved.

"Well, sir," I began cautiously. "I don't know about your morals, but my only sales experience has been as an exotic dancer." I continued, "Working in a gentlemen's club, I had to sell myself and my skill as an entertainer if I was going to be successful or make any money. It was 100% commission-based pay."

The CEO didn't even flinch, not a single change in his external disposition...no smile nor frown...no eyebrow raised or wrinkled. There was not a single indication that the information I just revealed would work for me or against me in securing the job. I left the interview that day nervous about what I had shared, and not knowing if I would hear from Promotus Advertising again.

After an extremely long week of waiting, I received a phone call from my friend. I was hired! I would be the office manager, and be paid $10 per hour. I reported for work a couple of weeks later, and sat down at my desk. There, scrolling across the screen in a continuous string, were the words that changed me. *"Your dynamic, radiant light is attractive to those who desire the truth."*

I sat there and stared at these words slowly gliding across the computer screen. I digested them one by one.

Your. (This is specific to me…not someone else's, but MINE!)

Dynamic. (Characterized by constant change, activity or progress.)

Radiance. (Light as emitted or reflected by something.)

Is. (Present tense…as in right now…today)

Attractive. (Pleasing or appealing to the senses.)

To. Those. Who. (Not everyone will be interested in what I have to offer.)

Desire. (A strong feeling of wanting to have something or wishing for something to happen.)

The. Truth. (Not those who desire a dance…or a good time…but the TRUTH!)

This was the most profound and personal message I had ever seen. I was honored that my friend would think to put such a statement as that on my computer to welcome me into the office. That simple and powerful statement set the tone for my entire experience there at Promotus Advertising, and for the rest of my life. I was excited about the new direction I was headed in, and my desire for spiritual food was growing.

One day I stopped my co-worker Domini as she was walking though the office.

"I'm looking for a church home," I told her. "Do you go to church?"

"No," she replied with a smile in her eyes. "I don't go to church."
She continued quickly. "I do go to fellowship, and you are more than welcome to join me whenever you would like!"

"Awesome!" I replied, excitedly. "What's the dress code?"

"Clean." Her answer was just like her, genuine and raw, yet completely unassuming.

Shortly after that discussion I attended my first fellowship. I had been to churches all my life, but this time was very different. I was being taught to understand the word, and to enjoy reading it. Slowly, I began to understand the magnitude of what Jesus Christ had accomplished for me, and how. And all that I learned in fellowship was being reinforced at work. There were so many lessons that year...some business and others spiritual...yet all rooted in God's Word.

One of the business lessons I learned was on the heels of my sub-par performance. I felt moved to talk to the CEO and let him know about my needs for more important and fulfilling work. The mundane, monotonous job of office manager no longer motivated me, and this lack of motivation (so I thought) resulted in missed deadlines and shabby results.

I pulled together every ounce of courage that I had, and marched confidently into that corner office.

"Excuse me Bruce," I said. "Can I talk to you for a minute?"

"Sure Steph," he replied. As usual with him, I couldn't tell what type of mood he was in. His cool demeanor was all at once calculating and inviting. But I had his ear for the moment, and needed to get to the point quickly.

"I think I know why my performance hasn't been up to par lately," I started. "I feel like I am capable of much more than I am doing, so more responsibility would actually help me perform at my best." There, I said it. I laid it out, and waited for him to see the genius in my thought process.

"Oh really?" His reply brought me back to reality.

"That is the exact opposite of what the Word says...grab the Bible." He directed over to the small conference table to the good book.

"Now, open it up to Luke 16:10," he directed, and I did. "Now, read it."

"Luke 16:10," I started reading the scripture. *He that is faithful in that which is least is faithful also in much; and he that is unjust in the least is unjust also in much.* I looked up from my reading.

"See, that is why we have to be careful." Bruce brought the lesson full circle.

"You are trying to tell me something that runs exactly opposite of what God's Word says. Why would I trust more of my business to you when you haven't demonstrated you can handle the little that I have given you?"

His voice and demeanor was firm, yet equally loving. We both knew he had taught me something in that moment. I walked away from that conversation and decided that from that day forward, I would be faithful with even the most minute tasks, no matter how insignificant they seemed.

My entire year working at Promotus Advertising would be like that. Full of learning. the word of God...the will of God...the love of God. In addition to working with like-minded believers, I continued to attend fellowship regularly. I took research classes to better understand God's Word and will for my life. I had never felt so sure of myself, and

I hungered and thirsted to know more. Slowly, I began to challenge my old ways of thinking, and started to build up my self-esteem.

The Lesson

My journey to that stage as an exotic dancer may have been well-scripted by the adversary, yet that experience was well used by God for my growth, learning, and promotion. I have never been a religious woman, but I have always believed in God. That year of daily work with believers coupled with in-depth study of the word of God kick-started my transformation into me. The real me.

I grew up believing that my physical traits were the best thing I had going. That my physical attributes and sexuality was my major commodity. But with my spiritual eyesight, I began to know a different thing. I began to see that I was God's workmanship. He called me out long before this earth was formed. He thoroughly equipped me to do his work. He made me with great intention and respect.

Who I am is exactly who God called me to be. Who I am is acceptable. I did not have to hide my truth in order to receive what God planned for me! Alone I was confused about who I was. God has always known who He made me to be. He was with me the entire time, even in the strip club. As He is with every one of his children. He knew my value before I did. He assigned my value to me.

Perhaps the single biggest spiritual battle I fought was the battle of self-condemnation. Self-condemnation is like a virus that gets into a computer and destroys it. It repeats lies over and over again until the subconscious mind accepts them as fact. "You ain't nothing!" it screams. "You don't deserve the best." "Why would anyone want you?" In my darkest days, I would wrap up in a blanket of self-loathing, sobbing uncontrollably and telling myself that I was damaged goods.

Each time I had to beat back those defeated thoughts with what God, through his word, says about me. You are wonderfully and fearfully made! You are more than a conqueror! At the same time I constantly reminded myself that nothing would separate me from the love of God. The more I confessed what the Word said, the more at peace I felt. The more calm...and eventually, more powerful.

Nay in all these things you are more than a conqueror through him that loved us!

I praise God because I am fearfully and wonderfully made! Your works are wonderful, and I know that full well!

There is therefore no condemnation to them which are in Christ Jesus...

The Future

I have a vision of returning to the stage. I can see it clearly. The room will be brightly lit, and the crowd filled with expectant excitement. The emcee will begin to announce:

"And now, I would like to introduce you to our keynote speaker for tonight's empowerment seminar. She hails from Indianapolis, IN as a certified 5D AIC coach, motivational speaker, and author. She is an instructor for the US Army Reserves, and a certified professional accountant licensed in the state of Indiana. She has an MBA, and has taught classes and workshops for the Business Owners Initiative, the Federal Women's Program, and Martin University. Joining us today to talk about "Answering the Call," please give a warm welcome to Coach Steph B!"

I stride out onto the stage and begin to bare myself again. This time, I bare my light, share my story, and see yet another glimpse of God's glory.

Betty Fisher

Betty Fisher's mission is to encourage all women to discover, grow, and go change the world. She is an entrepreneur, certified life coach, behavior consultant, empowerment speaker, host, facilitator, and emerging author.

Betty committed her life to Jesus Christ in the spring of 1990. She desires to experience the love of God through in-depth bible study, prayer, encouragement, dialogue, and relationships. Betty uses her platform as a catalyst to help mend the brokenness in relationships and families. She believes true healing and unity begins with confession, conversations, healthy communication, process, repentance, and prayer.

She has served in many organizations and outreaches including Berrien County Forgotten Man Ministry, a women's bible class in the Berrien County Jail and KPEP Correctional Facility. She visits local nursing homes and hospitals as an encourager through word and song ,is active with the Southwest MI Pinky Promise Organization and hosts a community symposium where men and women of various ethnicities, backgrounds, and locations discuss the challenges facing our families, communities, and churches. She uses her influence and platform to create unity, sister and brotherly love and support. Betty desires to use her platform to be a catalyst to help mend the brokenness in relationships and families.

*bio continued after story

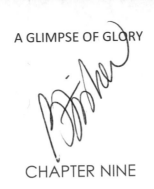

CHAPTER NINE

Pain to Purpose

L ife sure does have a way of challenging us to tap into our true identity, who God has destined and called us to be. If you've ever found yourself walking aimlessly through the mundaneness of life, not quite understanding the longing of your soul, to find and fulfill your life's purpose, perhaps this season of my journey may help you discover it.

Often we walk through our journey of life unclear of our true sense of self and purpose. Not realizing, more than often, our purpose is tied directly to our identity, our greatest source of pain, brokenness, and frustrations. Sickness, birth, or death even leads us there. But rest assured, God has a plan and an expected end for our lives.

For I know the thoughts that I think toward you, saith the LORD, thoughts of peace, and not of evil, to give you and expected end. Jeremiah 29:11 KJV.

If you've ever asked yourself these questions: "Who am I? Why am I here?" Perhaps connecting to your greatest source of pain, joy, or personal desires are clues. But, whatever you do, it's important to find and fulfill your life's purpose. It will bring you to your expected end and hope. Three years ago, I stumbled across a profound quote from Mark Twain. "The two most important days in your life are the day you are born and the day you find out why." Jesus knew his purpose, and it was seemingly tied to his greatest pain, betrayal, and redemption. Jesus told us repeatedly at several different times in the bible; *I must do the will of Him who sent me while it is day*...John 9:4 NKJV. *The thief does not come except to steal, and to kill, and to destroy. I have come that they may have life, and that more abundantly*, John 10:10 NKJV.

Even though Jesus didn't want to die, as he visited the place called Gethsemane, his soul was deeply grieved and distressed, to the point of death. Three times he visited the garden and prayed the cup of suffering would pass. He had to confront his flesh and his fate to do the will of his father who sent him. He came to save God's beloved people from their sins.

Have you experienced and reasoned with God about a pressing and uncomfortable, painful circumstance that's caused you to question your identity and purpose? Allow me to share an experience I once faced, in remembrance of Jesus in the garden; *My Father, if this cannot pass away unless I drink it, your will be done*, Matthew 26:42 NIV.

Every Season has Purpose

One Friday evening, routinely washing and conditioning my hair, I became extremely frustrated at the loss and thinning of it. As I combed, it began to repeatedly break and fall. I began to dread the mere thought of weekly maintenance and watching the seamlessly endless damage. As my frustration grew, I dreaded the process. It took me three years to grow it. I started searching for answers. In my research I didn't find any underlining health problems or contaminated water issues to place the blame. One week, in an instance, I reached my breaking point and couldn't take it anymore. Talking to myself, "No more of this, it's has to go, I've had it!" I decided to take the plunge and return to natural; without use of chemicals or transitioning. You now understand my frustration as I thought about the time and maintenance it took to grow healthy hair, now losing with minimal effort, raking, and combing.

Whom the Son sets free is free indeed. Nothing is worth losing yourself.

Once afternoon, during my weekly care and regimen, I called my husband into the bathroom. Under my direction he cut off the ponytail I placed on the top of my head, leaving short strands on the top and minimal hair on the sides. Nothing prepared me for the range of emotions that would spew afterward. As I cried, I thought, what did I just do myself? Am I going through menopause? I heard there's a range of emotions and symptoms women experience during this time. Perhaps that explained my problems. After I collected myself, I called and scheduled an appointment with my hair stylist for the following day.

Saturday morning arrives, stomach tingling with nerves, mentally preparing my mind a drastic change. I would no longer have long or chemical processed hair. There wasn't much hair minus the chemically altered hair. On my Saturday morning drive to the hair salon, I thought about the many styles I've worn, I never imagined, thought or ever considered I'd "big chop." This is an African American natural hair term related to the process of cutting off the relaxed or permed ends of one's hair when transitioning from processed chemically treated hair to what's naturally grown from the scalp. For some of you, you may wonder why would what seems to be a simple haircut have such emotions attached?

Much to My Surprise

Alarm clock rings, Sunday morning rise and shine! Turn on my morning coffee break; some good feet-stomping, hand clapping, head shaking, gospel music! Charged and ready to hear the word of God! Praise and worship music bumping and blasting throughout the house. Light breakfast, dressed, final touches on makeup, and one last look at the new do and out the door.

Walking into the foyer, I felt the cold, brisk breeze and air sweeping across the nape of my head and scalp. Shivering, instantly learning a con to short hair in the winter; a cold head. On the ride there I reflected on the last two days; my hair was armpit length, flowing, shiny, and beautiful. I hadn't completely recovered from the shock of the extreme makeover and unaware what lie ahead. There was no hair to keep me warm or hide my face as I'd grown accustomed to. Yet, I remain motivated from the pep talk and affirming words the day before from my husband and stylist. Running through my mind was his astonishment and noticeable attraction, it was difficult to deny. I saw it in his eyes, as he stared and gazed. Thinking of his last words the night before... *"Babe, out of all the styles you've worn you've never looked better, you can rock that, you're more beautiful now than ever, I love it... No, don't cover it up, wear it, you look great!"*

Twelve hours earlier, I stood in front of the mirror emotional and tearfully talking to myself about how unattractive I looked now and contemplating whether to wear or cover my teeny-weeny afro with a hat, scarf, or wig. I was known for versatility, usually wearing many different styles and looks. I thought to myself, its late fall, and cold, no one would know I was bald, by spring I'd have hair. As my husband looked on, he stood speechless in the bathroom doorway, leaning, with his hands on his hips, puzzled and helpless. He was trying to understand my spewing emotions, this wasn't the confident wife he knew. He'd just spoken of my radiant beauty, usually welcomed thankfully with a hug and kisses. Frozen, he stood watching what he couldn't comprehend and was unable to fix, as these are words he's shared countless times before.

Nothing would prepare me for my first encounter. I approached the information desk for a program and a distinguished, polished, dapper, elder African American gentleman, to my surprise, blatantly began to question and share his opinion on the noticeable change to my hair.

"Are you okay? Are you sick?" Before I was able to answer the first question, I was struck with one after another. "Why would 'yawl' do that to yourselves?

What do your husband thinks about that? 'Those' people are even affecting the church now. The bible says a woman's hair is her glory, why would you do that?" he asked. He looked at me with such disappointment.

I replied, "No sir, I'm not sick. I'm doing well as a matter of fact, never have I been better. And I don't know who 'those' people are. Yes, my husband loves and approves of it, and it's still my glory-short or not."

I picked up a program and quickly walked away into the sanctuary, as he mumbled, "I don't understand why a woman would purposely be bald-headed and wear nappy hair, I just don't understand it."

Trying to block out the offensive words spoken to me I walked to my seat. As usual, I lifted my hands and heart in during praise and worship time. Whispering under my breath praises and adoration to my God. I must admit it was difficult to stay focused. God's presences quickly swept through the sanctuary as the members in unity offered up praises to him.

Yet I was offended, vexed, shocked, and appalled. As I was trying to forget about just moments ago, I said to God, "This hurts, why he would say such a thing? I don't know, he's black too, with nappy hair, has he forgotten his roots...ugh. Am I supposed to just take it?" Tears began to stream down my face. As the rest of service proceeded, it was difficult to staying focused on the pastor's sermon. I'm sure it was great, as usual. But now, I'm in my feelings, becoming angry as the hour passed. I visualized and pondered thoughts running through my mind; I imagined going over to the elder gentlemen who hadn't displayed attributes of a gentlemen, nor a Christian.

I should walk right up to his seat and give him a piece of my mind before quickly heading out the door. He had ruined my day. The nerve of him, I thought.

Pretending to be interested while my husband and I reviewed bible passages our pastor was expounding I kept thinking, "I should've followed my first thought the night before. I told my husband I wanted to wear a wig, I shouldn't have listened to him in the first place, besides, I'm right, most of the time" I was fuming. All the while, my husband is completely unaware of my internal battle.

It's through your uniqueness God fulfills His purpose in you

Finally, what I've be impatiently anticipating; closing prayer and the benediction! Without a moment's notice, I was out of my seat and quickly headed to the exit door. I thought, I have to get out of here as fast as I can. I don't want anyone to see what 'may' appear to be apparent; anger and hurt. Just as I make it to the exit doors of the sanctuary, I hear my name ringing faintly from afar. Purposely ignoring it, I had no intention on stopping. I figured, by now if the first impression was cruel, I'm not going to wait around for anyone else to insult me. Just as I made it to the first exit, the voice became loud, I didn't see anyone and surely, wasn't going to turn around...

"Betty, wait, wait, wait... I saw you come in! Oh my god, you look amazing, what made you do it, who cut it, how does it feel, and may I touch it? And you look beautiful, like a queen!" I answered her questions as quickly as possible in an effort to get to the final exit door. It seemed many of my Caucasian and African American brothers and sisters began to surround me, astonished by my drastic transformation. Some of them complimented, others stared. For several weeks I answered the same questions repeatedly. I even thought of creating a sign for my front and back to answer all inquiring minds. It'd had gotten to the point of annoyance and irritation.

The Awakening

After a couple of months of wearing my afro hairstyle, I began to love the convenience it provided. However, I noticed many African Americans and members of my family weren't so accepting. I pondered; why wasn't natural hair embraced in the African American community, along with long-European styles? Why was it offensive? What threat or reminder did it pose? As weeks went by many others shared similar offensive questions and statements as the elder church member, and those who stood in the church exit doors. The findings were disheartening. I questioned whether or not this was how the African American community felt as a whole regarding their heritage. I wondered if I'd treated others who wore their hair natural in the same manner.

When I was a little girl, growing up in the seventies the black community appeared proud. I remember my parents, family, and friends wearing big afros, singing and dancing to James Brown lyrics, "Say it loud, I'm black and I'm proud!" When did that all change? Or was it empowerment or a movement for the times we faced in our country? I couldn't deny it, the negative words weighed heavily upon my heart. As a result, I began to deeply investigate my internal motives and way of being because it affected my peace, self-acceptance, self-image, and self-worth. I began to have moments of overwhelming, uncontrolled range and emotions; anguished feelings of inadequacy, as if I wasn't enough.

All Things Work Together

One morning as I prayed my emotions became increasingly uncontrollable, overflowing in my heart as I cried out to God. There were flashbacks of my childhood, a time I experienced great pain and suffered depression in silence; bullying in school caused me to become introvert, extremely shy, and timid. He began to reveal stains of my childhood, family, and marriage. The residue from rejection and severed relationships, which caused me to become withdrawn. I had never recalled a time in my childhood when I'd ever felt secure, or considered myself to be pretty. Often teased and bullied about my big buck teeth and acne, I became uncomfortable speaking in front of others and my class. Strange to say, I was accustomed to negativity, criticism, and discipline. As many of us who grew up with parents from the south, it was the norm to receive stern discipline, and sparingly was affection and affirmation. I was anguished and disappointed at my reflection, as I began to argue with God, "I thought I was over this, I thought I was past rejection and how others said and made me feel. Why you would bring this to me now, why now?"

He began to speak into my spirit, *"My daughter, I created you in my image, you're not a mistake, and I created your uniqueness. I created your innermost being; and knitted you together in your mother's womb and every strand of hair on your head I numbered and will use for my glory. You are fearfully and wonderfully made in my image and likeness. I make no mistakes. I created you for me. I knew you. I chose and appointed you for this time."*

What a priceless reminder from such a loving and sovereign God. Never had I felt so beautiful, loved, and accepted. His words were the dawning of a new day, a new perspective, an awakening, and clarity. The tears and embracing love of the Father washed and cleansed my soul. As I gathered myself, it was becoming clear; the purpose of losing my hair was to see myself in his image, not the labels and standards of the world, and those of my parents or ancestors. I vowed to take God at his word and never allow opinions of others to incarcerate me again. God's word became the final authority, no condemnation. The extent Jesus went to prove my worth, and God's love for us, I'd never question again.

God deemed you worthy before you were ever conceived

Greater love hath no man than this that a man would lay His life down for His friends. John 15:13 KJV.

For His Glory

To prove my self-love and self-acceptance, I personally challenged myself and promised for a year, in the dead, freezing-cold of winter to honor, celebrate, and embrace my uniqueness and heritage by wearing my natural hair uncovered. I vowed to never allow others' opinions to incarcerate my liberty and authentic self. Whom the Son sets free is free indeed. Nothing is worth losing yourself.

"Your strength is in your uniqueness. If you lose your sense of who you are, you have nothing in which to return. If you don't discover your passions, purpose, and power, then you will pursue the roles assigned by other people's script. If you lose your strength to get along with others, then you have nothing original to offer this new world of possibilities," T.D. Jakes.

It's through your uniqueness God fulfills His purpose in you.

Although I had gained a freedom and was eager to share, I realized the negative stigmas in our culture concerning natural hair was historical, and we were deeply scarred as a result of psychologically damaging words spoken to our ancestors which were passed down through generations, negatively impacting an entire race and culture, devaluing ourselves and unique heritage. I realize the historical and the self-inflicting pain has yet to be healed. The pain of words, brutality and oppression, infecting our self-acceptance and love for each other; from our kinkynappy hair and texture, various hues, education, background, status, fatherless homes, divorce rate, poverty, broken and estranged families. It's far time we heal the deep wounds and labels placed upon us. We need to reclaim our power, authority, and embrace and celebrate our rich, unique culture. God has called me to be a catalyst for the process of healing through healthy dialogue regarding the stigmas and brokenness that continues to plague and destroy the unity of humanity, of all mankind.

According to His Purpose

The purpose of my pain was never about my hair, it was about self-acceptance and embracing God's unique design. It was to inspire, empower, and encourage, perhaps a timid, frightened, shy, insecure, unsure, rejected, fatherless girl or boy, man or woman, with beautiful-hued naked skin, nappy hair or silk tresses, the rejected, orphaned, and ostracized.

From your laughter to your smile, to the joys and pains of your heart, God deemed you worthy before you were ever conceived …you are 'so' loved to the extent of death, Jesus redeemed you. Your worth has never depended upon acceptance from others but from the two greatest loves of all; God and yourself. God's love and acceptance trumps labels. God's thoughts of you are good, and not of evil. He's blessed, with no regrets. You are uniquely, authentically, and perfectly poised to change the world.

Endnotes:
Jeremiah 29:11 KJV

*Betty's bio continued

She believes true healing and unity begins as a result of confession, conversations, healthy communication, process, repentance, and prayer.

Betty is a native of Utica, New York and currently resides in Benton Harbor, MI. She has been married for thirteen years to her husband and has three children.

For I know the thoughts that I think toward you, saith the Lord, thoughts of peace, and not of evil, to give you an expected end.
Jeremiah 29:11, KJV.

Sabrinna Stennette

Sabrinna is a native of Indianapolis, IN. She obtained her degree in Organizational Leadership from Purdue University and Masters of Business Administration from Indiana Wesleyan University. Sabrinna is a Playwright, contributing author in *A Peace of Me; My Journey of Authenticity*, and community activist. She is an AIC Graduate of 5D-Authentically Me and plans to become a public speaker.

Sabrinna is the mother of Andre Stennette-Harrod, a Ball State student who was gunned down violently on Father's Day, June 17, 2012. As a surviving parent, she looks at herself as victorious, not a victim. Having found her voice, Sabrinna speaks out in the community against violence promoting positive programs through her son's nonprofit organization, Play It 4Ward Sports and Entertainment Co.

Sabrinna Stennette also keeps her son's legacy alive though other platforms such as hosting "Syndicated Village" radio show on Dejoi Soul Café (www.dejisoul.com) and participates on panel discussions addressing violence in our community. She is a member of the Community Response Team (CRT) for the Mayor's office. Sabrinna plans to continue being a voice for surviving parents who have not yet found theirs. Sabrinna is a member of New Life
bio continued at end of story

CHAPTER TEN

Breaking Up With Fear

Be ye transformed by the renewing of your mind.

A s a ten-year-old girl, I had no problem climbing trees and chasing bugs. My mother used to wake up every morning at 4:30 A.M. She used to always say, "It's the early bird that catches the worm." I took that so literally that I would wake up around 7 a.m. every morning in the summer because I wanted the catch worms, crickets, butterflies, and any other bug I could find. My sister Kim and I would go fishing with my dad, and I had no problem handing him the bait to put on the pole. One day, when I was 12 or 13 years old, I saw an interesting bug I had never seen before wiggling about two branches up on the tree in our yard. I decided to chase after it and before I knew it I had fallen out of a tree, landed on my back, and almost bite my tongue off.

The next day I woke up around 10 a.m., I no longer had the desire to catch worms, crickets, butterflies, and any other bugs. I held on to my tears and overnight fear crept in and stole my love. From that day forward, I allowed fear to court me, comfort me, and control me which made it easy to hide from everything. I became very shy and fear prevented me from talking to people. I had opportunities to go away on scholarship to college but fear wouldn't allow me to go too far from home so I turned them down. I began to feel like leadership and servitude was my purpose but fear said, "Who would follow you?"

Just like any relationship where there is no give only take, my relationship with fear became dysfunctional. What was comfortable and familiar became the very thing that hurt me. I allowed fear to drain the destiny out of me and steal things from me that I thought I would never get back. I took the fears of my childhood into my adulthood and it literally stopped me from growing, progressing, and evolving to the person God called me to be.

Courting Fear

Marianne Williamson says it best in her poem, A Return to Love: Reflections on the Principles of "A Course in Miracles." In it she states, "Our deepest fear is not that we are inadequate. Our deepest fear is that we are powerful beyond measure. It is our light, not our darkness that most frightens us. We ask ourselves, 'Who am I to be brilliant, gorgeous, talented, and fabulous?' Actually, who are you not to be? You are a child of God."

I can't remember a time in my life when it didn't frighten me to let my light shine. No matter how qualified I was I would never take a role that would bring attention to myself because I didn't want people to notice me. Fear made me insecure and lack self-worth. I was embarrassed when people complimented me so I hid behind glasses and weight. I wanted to be a public speaker but fear had me so paralyzed that I couldn't even get my thoughts together. I wanted to be a college professor, but fear had me feeling like I wasn't brilliant enough. Every day I came home to find my fear on my couch chillaxing in front of the big screen TV watching the football game. It had no intentions of leaving because I allowed fear of situations and things to be front and center in every aspect of my life.

Fear had all my attention, but I know I am not alone. Studies show that 63 Million Americans have been diagnosed with fear (phobia).[1]

There are two basic types of fear which are:

1) **Fear of an object**: when you are afraid of small animals, snakes, insects, closed spaces, flying in planes, etc.

2) **Fear of situations**: when you are afraid of social settings like meeting new people, giving a speech, or talking to your boss. Traumatic events are what often time trigger your relationship with fear.[2]

Because so many people live their lives in fear, it has become our greatest enemy. Fear is just the devil's device to keep you from your destiny. It is crippling and debilitating, and will steal time, destiny, and purpose. If you live your life in fear, you will look up one day to see your whole life passed by and you have nothing to show for it.

The scariest fact that I found about fear is that it is contiguous. That means that the impact of fear runs far deeper than you know. Living a fear driven life not only affects you, but it can affect your kids, friends, and love ones. I am a witness that it can even become generational.

To this day, I don't like cats because my mom was afraid of cats. When she was small, a cat jumped on her and made her fall off the porch and she busted her lip. Ever since that day every time she saw a cat, her world literally stopped. I watched her time and time again run, scream, and cry every time she saw a cat. Even though I have never personally had a bad experience with cats, I am very uneasy around them.

I can't tell you the countless number of times I allowed fear to come back into my life and each time it stayed longer than I intended. I walked around looking okay on the outside by smiling, laughing, and faking it on the inside. When I began to unravel myself from fear's ugly web, I was completely confused and lost. I realized that fear wasn't making me happy, it was making me numb.

For so long my fears were a response to the tragedies of my life. Since the day my son was murdered I would ask, "God, why did you choose me to carry this burden?" Then he answered with a quote I saw on a bracelet that stated, "I was given this life because I am strong enough to handle it." What was I missing when I submitted to fear and forgot whose I was?

Let Me Introduce You to Someone New

Friends and family in your life don't want to see you in a bad relationship because they want what's best for you. Often they take you out and try to introduce you to someone new who will show you the way you should be treated. But when you've been in a dysfunctional relationship for so long, sometimes you are so damaged that when someone tries to give you what you deserve it's hard for you to recognize a good thing when it's sitting in front of you.

God gives us constant reminders of who He is and how much He loves us through His word. His word is designed to lavish His love on us by connecting with Him. And even though I'm broken and messed up, He allows me to experience healing, love, and peace.

Paul tells us, *For by Him all things were created that are in heaven and that are on earth, visible and invisible, whether thrones or dominions or principalities or powers. All things were created through Him and for Him.* Colossians 1:16, 17.

These verses say that He who created, controls; He who authored life is authority over life. The same God who spoke the universe into existence oversees counseling sessions and chemotherapy. No wonder God asks, "To whom shall I be equal?" Isaiah 40:25.

Life, with all its fearful debris, rotates around the fixed axis of God's sovereignty. "This is my Father's world," the hymn says — not mine, not the government's, not the surgeon's who will be operating in the morning. This doesn't mean that bad things won't happen, but that God will tell us what to do when we don't know what to do.

The Thing about being Brave is it doesn't come with the absence of fear and hurt. Bravery is the ability to look fear and hurt in the face and say move aside, you are in my way.
Melissa Tumino

He'll impress us with proper actions and attitudes. The Holy Spirit instructs, convicts, and guides John 16:13. We can count on Him to give us sanity in the midst of panic. And we can count on God to work bad into good if we love Him, Romans 8:28

We lose sight of this because fear of the future blurs our perception. One bad report from the blood test, a meltdown on Wall Street, and God shrinks in our fear-skewed perception. But the truth is if we remember our Creator, *we* shrink — not God.

His word is designed to lavish His love on us by connecting with Him

When I consider your heavens, the work of your fingers. What is man that You are mindful of him, and the son of man that You visit him? Psalm 8:3, 4.

Confidence in God's control puts us at ease no matter what looms ahead. Jesus, for example, knew exactly what suffering awaited Him in Jerusalem. Yet He didn't shrink from the future; He led the way to Jerusalem (Mark 10:32). Jesus knew that the plan God set in motion after the Fall had triumph written between the lines of tragedy, and that even Pilate merely fulfilled a role God had given him (John 19:10, 11).

Despite what we see or can't see, what we feel or dread, God's world has purpose and plan. Mistakes and mishaps do not have the final word. God uses our adversities and situations to give us a glimpse of His glory because that is when He can show up and show out. God has the final word; so, if I can just remind myself of Philippians 4:19, "My God shall supply all my needs according to his riches in glory." When I allowed God into my life it gave me a different perspective. It is time to flip the script on fear.

Breaking Up with Fear: It's not you it's me

God has given us all a purpose, an assignment before we were even born.

For I know the plans I have for you, declares the LORD, plans to prosper you and not to harm you, plans to give you hope and a future. Jerimiah 29:11.

It is our obligation as Christians to walk in God's purpose and plan for us. When we are purpose driven, that is when we get a glimpse of His glory.

Moreover, God is the source of all good things. He actually shares his glory with us. When we receive his plentiful gifts with gratitude, when we use them to enhance his honor, when we acknowledge Him as the source of all goodness, then we are glorifying Him.

I used to hear the elders of the church sing a song that asked the question, who wouldn't serve a God like mine? And I didn't know what they meant at the time, but every day that I wake up with a good portion of my health and strength, with purpose and destiny that He specifically chose me to carry out, and with His word as my shield to protect and guide me through any thing I may fear, I get a glimpse of His glory.

In Psalms 23:4 God promised me that even though I walk through the darkest valley, I will fear no evil, for He is with me; His rod and His staff they comfort me. As we walk in His purpose, people begin to see Him through us and God is glorified. When men see a glimpse of God in us, it makes them want to say, "How can I get some of what you have?"

Let's keep it real. Fear will always be at the front door waiting to get back in, but we don't have to let fear back in. We can stand on the promises of God and know that our God, Jehovah-Nissi, will be our banner and give us the victory over fear. You can point your finger in the face of fear and shout with authority, "FEAR, you don't live here anymore! I gotta let you go."

There comes a pivotal moment in every relationship where you experience a paradigm shift. You must determine whether you are going to move forward or let the past drag you back.

I found someone who loves me unconditionally and treats me the way I should be treated. He makes me giddy, because when I think about His goodness I can't help but smile. He is on my mind from the time I wake up in the morning until I go to sleep at night. Even in the midnight hour when I call Him, He answers. I trust Him with my life because He is the giver of life. He wants what's best for me; therefore, He continues to show me that I am wanted and valued through His word and His actions. His word tells me that the very hairs on our heads are all numbered.

So don't be afraid; you are more valuable to God than a whole flock of sparrows.[4] He tells me that I am fearfully and wonderfully made.[5] Every day I wake up to the birds chirping His love song to me. He loves me so much that He hung the moon and cast the stars in the sky. He is my strength when I am weak and His grace covers and protects me daily from all hurt, harm and danger. God is everything to me.

There is no greater love than God's love for me, so I strive to get back to that **fearless, brave** girl who chased bugs up the tree. She was **faithful** and **dedicated** to her purpose. And even though she fell out the tree, she now knows she can get back up again, dust herself off, and press toward the mark of the high calling which is in Jesus Christ. As Christians and representatives of God, we have to be **strong** and **courageous** knowing that when we are, believers and unbelievers alike can see through us a glimpse of His glory.

A Prayer for Break the Stronghold of Fear
Dear God,

I want to first ask that you please forgive me for not trusting you. I ask you to change me and make me whole. I need your help to break the stronghold of fear on my life. I cling to you knowing that you will never leave or forsake me. Please strengthen me where I am weak and help me to hold on. I declare and decree that I will live the life you have planned for me and a life reflective of your excellence. Let your perfect love cast out my fears. **I choose you!** I ask that you provide me with a clear, concise purpose. I will stand on your promise that you have not given me the spirit of fear, but of power and of love and of a sound mind (2 Timothy 1:7). I know that I am protected by your love and covered by your grace. Grant me the courage to walk in my brilliant, gorgeous, talented, and fabulous truth so that everyone who encounters me can see a glimpse of your glory.
Amen

Endnotes:
http://psychcentral.com/lib/facts-about-phobias/
Langton, Sherri.
Facing   the   Future   Without   Fear,   from:
http://www1.cbn.com/facing-future-without-fear
The   High   Calling.   What   is   God's   Glory,   from:
https://www.theologyofwork.org/the-high-calling/daily-reflection/what-gods-glory?
Luke 12:7 NLT

---

*Sabrinna's bio continued
Worship Center where she serves on the Altar Workers and Dance ministries. She is also a member of Delta Sigma Theta Sorority, Inc. Sabrinna's foundational life scriptures are Psalms 23, Jeremiah 29:11 and Romans 8:28 and she has adopted her son Andre's motto for life, "Turn down for what?" She gets up every day and lives life intentionally.

Lift up your heads, O gates, And be lifted up, O ancient doors, That the King of glory may come in! Who is the King of glory? The LORD strong and mighty, The LORD mighty in battle.
Psalm 24:7-8

Nicole Evans

Nicole is a gifted, motivational, inspirational, and transformative speaker that is passionate about helping and coaching others to achieve their dreams and live in purpose.

Nicole is the host of the *Winning in Life Today* talk show that airs three times a week on the MaxLife Christian Women's Network at www.maxlifeitv.org.

As a 20 year-veteran of the US Army, Nicole received in-depth leadership training which she now uses to influence others to accomplish their personal missions in life. After serving 18 years in the military, Nicole was selected for promotion to Sergeant Major, the highest enlisted rank in the U.S. Army. This was a very pivotal moment and great accomplishment in her career. After much prayer and consideration Nicole decided to turn down the promotion, retire, and enter corporate America. As a certified Senior Human Resources Professional (SPHR, SHRM-SCP), certified DISC Human Behavior Consultant, and a certified Life Coach with a Master's Degree from the University of Oklahoma, Nicole has coached and mentored junior, senior, and executive leaders in both the government and private sectors.

Nicole's winning attitude has inspired audiences across the US, Latin America, and Germany. Her motto when speaking is the three B's; **"Be Brief, Be Brilliant, Be Gone"**.

CHAPTER ELEVEN

Say Yes to Destiny's Call

I STILL HAVE SOMETHING LEFT TO OFFER. I STILL
HAVE MORE TO GIVE.
I STILL HAVE SOMETHING LEFT TO OFFER. I STILL
HAVE MORE TO GIVE.

Somewhere along this life's journey, I realized I had something more to offer this world, more than what I had already given, more than the 20 years I served in the US Army, more than the time I spent in corporate America, and more than the faithful service I rendered to the various ministries I served.

I'm unable to provide you with the specific date and time I had this awakening; however, I can tell you that somewhere between the age of 45 and 46, something happened. I'm at a loss for words as to how to describe exactly what happened, but I just know that something happened. If I had to attribute this awakening to some "thing," I would have to attribute it to that point in my life where I could no longer settle for the status quo, that point in my life I could no longer remain in the box that I allowed man to put me in. I can attribute it to that moment I made the decision to answer destiny's call.

When destiny is calling you, your place of comfort becomes uncomfortable.

There was a period of time in my life when I felt like this can't be all there is to life. As I began to evaluate my life and reflect on the various things I accomplished, I felt it was good, but at the same time I felt like it was not good enough. I went down the list:

Master's Degree ✓
Wonderful Marriage ✓
Great Career ✓
Beautiful Home ✓
Dream Car✓

Although I had checked the box in a lot of areas, I still felt unproductive and unfruitful. I felt there was something down on the inside saying you still have more to give. To those of you reading this story, my prayer is that if you ever experience the feelings of having nothing left to offer, feelings of being unproductive, and/or unfruitful, you will remember my story and be encouraged to know that there is MORE inside of you. You still have purpose; there are still untapped gifts inside of you, waiting to be used and shared with others. You still have the power and the ability to be all that God has called you to be. Just say yes to destiny's call, and catch a glimpse of what He has already prepared for you. Destiny's journey will come with its twists and turns, peaks and valleys, but I believe it will lead you to a place you were meant to be.

Let The Journey Begin

When soldiers are in formation and have to move from point A to point B, they are given the command *Forward march* in order to move to their next destination. As they are marching they are sometimes given the command *Mark time march*. When the command *Mark time march* is given, the soldiers begin to march in place, and their forward progress comes to a halt. The interesting thing about this command is the soldier is still making all of the marching movements; their arms are swinging back and forth, and their feet are moving up and down, but there is no forward progress; they remain in the same spot. They are making all of the necessary movements that would progress them forward; however, it's as if they're standing still.

There was a time in my life when I was at mark time march, I was doing a whole lot of movement, and involved in a whole lot of different activities, but I wasn't going anywhere. I was not making any forward progress in my life. I was in the same place, looking at the same people, saying to myself there has to be more. While I became comfortable and complacent at march time march for awhile, I still had the compelling feeling of there is more for me to do. This compelling feeling begin to overwhelm me so much so that I begin to get restless and uncomfortable.

I began to have thoughts, dreams, and visions about starting my own business. As these thoughts occurred to me, I began to write them down on paper and tuck them away. My thoughts would not let me rest. As I went about my day to day life, doing my normal routine, my thoughts became louder and louder. I could no longer focus on the things I was supposed to be doing, because I was distracted by the thoughts of starting a talk show, and becoming a motivational speaker that would inspire, motivate, and encourage others to live a winning life.

Often times when destiny is calling you, it is calling you to a place that you feel you are not equipped and/or prepared to go.

I thought to myself, a talk show host? I don't have a journalism background; I don't have anyone to interview. Better yet, who will want to sit down and talk to me, and oh by the way what are we going to talk about? Where am I going to get the equipment? The more questions I asked the more answers I received. It was as if I was receiving download after download of what I was supposed to do, and what my new journey in life would be. As I received glimpses of what my future would be and the things I would be doing, I became restless, bored, unsatisfied, and uncomfortable with the things I was doing at the time.

Although I became restless and no longer interested with what I was doing, I stayed committed to it, because that's what was expected of me. I thought about what people would think of me if I no longer did what they expected me to do. What would people say about me if I no longer conformed to their mold of me? So, instead of disappointing others and shattering their expectations of me, I ignored destiny's call and continued to *mark time march.*

Often times we try to conform to images and expectations that are not congruent with the image in which we were created. When this occurs it will cause you to have a distorted image of not only who you are, but also of whom you are to become. In order to move forward you most let go of others expectations and opinions.

Forward March

After another year of being at *mark time march,* I begin to get very irritable, easily agitated, and frustrated with what I was doing. Although I was in motion, making a lot of movement and doing a lot of things, I still felt like I was unfruitful and unproductive. Don't get me wrong - I had a good life, great marriage, great job; everything was good, except internally I knew I had more to offer than what I was currently doing.

One day while sitting on my couch I internally heard the command, *Go, do it now.* To me that was my marching orders, my *forward march* command to move forward in spite of what others would think or say. I got up from my couch, wrote a little script, pulled out my JVC camcorder, my husband did the recording and I posted it on Facebook. That was the launch of my talk show, *Winning In Life Today.* I didn't consult with anyone; I didn't ask anyone's permission or seek anyone's opinion; I simply obeyed my command.

When you answer destiny's call, some people will question your motives, and feel you have a hidden agenda. Move forward in spite of others' opinions about what you are doing.

Breaking away from the status quo and other people's expectations of you is very difficult, because we often long for the acceptance and approval of others. When I said yes to destiny and obeyed the command to move forward, it also meant I was saying no to the expectations or plans of what others had in mind for me.

As I moved forward with *Winning In Life Today*, I began to experience happiness and excitement that I had not previously experienced. I was learning new things, I was meeting and seeing new people, I was finally doing something in which I felt I was not only making a difference, but forward progress was being made. I began to discover new talents and gifts I never knew were inside of me.

The more I worked on my new company (my baby), the bigger the vision became. I developed my mission and vision statement. I created a vision board with images of how I saw myself in the future. What started off as just a simple Facebook post, moved forward to a YouTube channel, and after a few months I was ready for more. To my surprise the talk show was picked up by a Christian women's network, MaxLife ITV. Not only did they give me one slot, but three slots for the show to air three times a week. Please keep in mind the person with no background in broadcast journalism now has a show airing three times a week. The person with no background in journalism or television now creates, edits, and produces her own shows.

When destiny is calling you, your place of comfort becomes uncomfortable

When you say yes to destiny, destiny has a way of providing you with everything you need.

Reach Beyond

After a year and a half of doing the talk show, I still felt like I had something more to offer, something more of myself to give. Although I was feeling happy and excited about what I was doing, there was still a sense of confinement. There was still a feeling of being in a box, and my reach to impact others limited. What was limiting me? What was holding me back?

As I once again looked at my life and identified my gifts, I realized that the parts of my life that were not involved with work or family were involved with the church. Any gifts or talents I had, I used them in the church. Whether it was writing, producing and directing plays, or singing in the choir, or leading a ministry, I was only utilizing my gifts in the church. I came to realize that my metaphorical box was the church. I came to realize that my feelings of having something more to offer was actually a calling and a yearning to reach beyond the four walls of the church. It was a call and a yearning to reach beyond the traditions that were now making the church ineffective. It was time for me to change my "modus operandi" as it relates to ministry and how I serve people, and lead others to Christ.

Destiny will cause you to shift outside of the norm; which will cause conflict with those not ready nor willing to shift from the norm.

As I looked at the life of Jesus, I realized that He also operated outside of the box. The way Jesus did ministry and the way he served others was unorthodox, unconventional, and nontraditional. It caused others to be at odds with Him. Yet, He did not allow the critics of his methodology to stop Him from moving forward. Once, I received this revelation that was my light bulb moment, it was my awakening.

The Awakening

An awakening is like scales falling from your eyes. Although you've had sight all this time, an awakening causes you to see things from a whole different perspective. There is a shifting in the mindset that occurs. An awakening causes an evolution and a transformation to take place, and the person you've transformed into is barely recognizable to those that still see you in the box.

As I received the download of what I should do next as it relates to the vision of *Winning In Life Today*, I was once again excited, and ready to move forward. I was ready to launch and share the vision with others. As I shared my vision with others about reaching beyond the four walls of the church, I received mixed reviews; for the most part people were happy and excited. However, there were some who did not receive it very well, and were not supportive in the way I wanted to receive support. This caused me some concern and angst. Once again I was seeking the approval of others, and wanted to meet the expectations of others. Now, if this were a few years earlier, I would have allowed the lack of support to derail me, divert me, delay me, and/or stop me. This time something happened; this time there was something different about me and I was determined that I was not going to allow anyone to stop me from moving forward. I realized that I was created to be fruitful, to multiply, to have dominion, replenish, and subdue upon this earth. I realized that I was a creative being with many gifts inside of me to share with the world. I realized that I had something left to offer, and something more to give. I realized that what I had to offer could no longer remain in a box, and I could no longer settle for the status quo. Was this an easy decision? No. Was it the right decision? Yes.

My decision to say yes to destiny and to break out of the box left me in a strange place. I felt like people begin to distance themselves from me, and look at me strangely. I felt like conversations were going on about me that may have skewed others' opinions of me and about what I was doing. I felt like I was an outcast among people that once embraced me. I must emphasize this is the way I felt; it doesn't mean it was necessarily true, but it is the way I felt and the way I perceived things to be. I constantly had to tell myself, *Nicole, you got this. Keep your head up, keep a smile on your face, and walk through the crowd with confidence. You haven't done anything wrong.*

Your destiny is waiting for you to say YES.

Sometimes destiny will cause you to question whether you made the right move.

Don't second guess your yes. As an Army recruiter, I often had recruits say yes to join the Army and becoming a soldier. They were so excited about their decision to join and could not wait to leave. However, many second guessed their decision after receiving negative feedback from family and friends. What they were once excited about and ready to pursue was now deflated, devalued, and dismissed.

When it comes to saying yes to destiny, I want you to remember these four points from the movie *The Pursuit of Happyness:*

- Don't ever let anyone tell you, you can't do something. Not even those closest to you.
- You have to protect your dream.
- Don't allow the limitations of others to stop you. Moreover, don't allow your own perceived limitations about yourself to stop you.
- If you want something, go get it. PERIOD!

Pure Happiness

Your destiny is waiting for you to say YES. When I said yes to destiny's call to reach beyond the four walls of the church it started with a thought. After the thought, I begin to form mental images about what I was called to do and what it would look like. I took those mental images and begin to articulate what I saw in my mind. Not only did I talk about it, but I also applied action to what I was saying. Remember, your thoughts, plus words, plus action, equals manifestation.

When the full manifestation of what I said yes to was visible for all to see, it was beyond what I even imagined. As I looked at what was once a thought in my mind now in its physical manifestation, I realized that this was only a glimpse of what God has in store for me. As I looked at the lives that were touched and the impact that was made, I realized that it was truly the Lord's doing and it was marvelous in my eyes. At the end of the day my yes to destiny put me in a place of pure happiness. At the end of the day it was true that I still had something left to offer, and something more to give. Everyone that was supposed to be there in that moment was present; everyone's support I wanted to have was there in full support. Was it easy? No! Was it worth it? You bet!

Deuteronomy 28:8 says *when you obey God he guarantees a blessing on everything you do.* When you obey God and say yes to destiny, nothing you imagine will be restrained from you. How long will you contemplate destiny's call? Say yes and catch a glimpse of the glory God wants to reveal in your life. 1 Corinthians 2:9 says *No eye has seen, no ear has heard, and no mind has imagined what God has prepared for those who love him.*

YOU STILL HAVE SOMETHING LEFT TO OFFER, YOU STILL HAVE MORE TO GIVE.

YOU STILL HAVE SOMETHING LEFT TO OFFER, YOU STILL HAVE MORE TO GIVE.

YOU STILL HAVE SOMETHING TO PURSUE. GO GET IT!

Endnotes
Gen 1:28, KJV
Ps 118:23, KJV
Deut 28:8, NLT
1 Cor 2:9, NLT

Terrell & Keri Sarver

Terrell and Kerri shared a common childhood experience, now they are eager to share how God used those situations to bring them together.

Terrell L. Sarver was born, raised and resides in Indianapolis, Indiana and is the oldest of five siblings. He has been married to his wife, Kerri Sarver for seven years and is the father of four children. Kirstee, Justus, London, and Rylee.

They attend Life Restoration Church. Terrell is an active ordained elder and is currently pursuing a degree in ministry leadership at Advance Ministry Institute.

Terrell owns and operates a commercial financing firm located in Indianapolis, IN, specializing in lending money to small businesses and start-ups, real estate financing, church financing, unsecured, and secured business line of credit and working capital. Terrell has owned this company for over five years.

Terrell has several certifications, in foreclosure, first time home buyer, credit education, and financial literacy.

Terrell has an eBook titled: *Be Your Own Credit Counselor.* Terrell and Kerri Sarver's upcoming release: *From Death to Life!* a story about how God resurrected their marriage, finances, self-esteem, and lives.
bio continued after story

CHAPTER TWELVE

Broken, But Restored for His Glory!

Kerri's Story

M y life began as a controversy. I was born on November 30, 1973 to an African American woman and a Caucasian male. My mother was only 17 when she had me and married my father, soon divorced and abandoned to raise me as a single mother within two years. My mother and I moved in with my grandmother before I started kindergarten. My mother worked a late-night shift at a factory so my grandmother would get me ready for school in the mornings. My uncle lived in the home with my grandmother too.

My mother never remarried and pretty much struggled as a young single mother but she took me to church on Sundays. I attended vacation bible school, bible study and children's church. The Bible says *Train up a child in the way he should go: and when he is old, he will not depart from it.* Proverbs 22:6. I developed a relationship with the Lord at a young age. I was baptized at age nine and loved singing praise and worship. Despite our challenges, I felt loved, secure, and somewhat spoiled since I was the only child.

By the time I was about 10, I realized my mother had a drinking problem. On many occasions, she would be so drunk she had to be carried in our home by her peers or family members. Some mornings, my grandmother had a hard time waking my mother from her sleep and that always startled me because I thought she was dead.

Due to the lack of a father in my life and the chaos in our home, God sent loved ones in my life to fill in the gap and show me another way of life. The Bible depicts God to be *A father to the fatherless, and a judge of the widows, is God in his holy habitation*, Psalms 68:5.

My grandfather lived in Los Angeles and invited me for summer breaks. It was then that he taught me responsibility, financial literacy, and the importance of education. God also put women in my life to show me class, virtuousness, and dignity. I even had the opportunity to have a friend whose mother would include me in all their family gatherings. I would watch her clean, cook, and take care of her children with excellence. All the qualities I admired as a young girl, but didn't experience in my own home, God intentionally placed around me.

By my teen years, my uncles' daily weed smoking habit increased to a crack cocaine addiction. He would smoke this drug in the basement of our home. It always smelled like burnt plastic and my little neighbor friends would come inside our home and ask, "What is that terrible smell?" Soon I was too embarrassed to have anyone come into our home due to my grandmother's lack of control and discipline in her home, my uncles drug addiction, and my mother's drinking problem. I wanted to stay away as much as possible. I found myself befriending peers with the same unhealthy behaviors in their homes. We would rip and run the streets seeking entertainment to hide our pain.

At age 16, we were still living with my grandmother. Though she never required any structure, obedience, or respect in her home, she worked very hard as a supervisor at the US Postal Service and modeled fiscal responsibility. What I didn't realize as a child was that God placed loved ones around me to sow valuable qualities in my life that I would eventually tap into as an adult. If you dig deep, you may find greatness even in those who brought the dysfunction into your life.

At 18 I followed my high school boyfriend to a junior college in the suburbs of Chicago. Three years later I transferred to IUPUI and became pregnant at age 22 and had my first baby girl, Justus. My boyfriend and I grew apart and he remained involved in our daughter's life as a great father. It took several years to get my bachelor's degree. I married my first husband at 28 and it only lasted three years. During that marriage, I had my second baby girl, London. As I reflect on that season of my life, I am reminded that God will never take anything away from you without the intention of replacing it with something better for you.

During the divorce, I became serious about my salvation. One evening while lying in my bed I was feeling so distraught about the failure of my marriage, being a single woman with two kids, and for falling for the tricks, lies and deceit. I was in so much pain and anguish about the mistakes I made in life. These thoughts kept whirling over and over in my mind until suddenly I began to cry out "Jesus help me!" It was that night that Jesus became so real to me. I had a spiritual encounter with my heavenly father. I began reading the Word again, attending intercessory prayer, and even joined a ministry. I had such a passion and fire for the Lord. I developed strength to get certification in real estate, which was something I had always wanted to do. I forgave myself and my ex-husband, choosing to encourage and cooperate with him so he could be a father to our daughter, London.

A couple years later while working one day, I stopped in a mortgage company to solicit my real estate business. I ran into a gentleman that I recognized from church. We had a great conversation that lead to a budding friendship. Meeting at church led to praying on the phone together, to dating, to marriage and less than two years later, the birth of our daughter, Rylee. Seven years later this fine gentleman is my life partner and continues pushing me to be the woman God has called me to be.

Terrell's Story

In my life, I had to endure a lot of hurt, pain, and disappointments. I can remember as a teenager I had a perfect picture for my life. I had this dream that I would graduate from high school, attend and graduate college, have a promising career, a loving wife, and love God, all by the age of 26. As I share my story, you'll realize very quickly that God had another route for me.

I was a young man who was raised in the church. I knew that I had a call on my life, but I didn't know what to do with it. I didn't even know who I could talk to about it. I was a church baby. My great grandmother kept us in church; it was all I knew. So much so that my brother and I would get teased and laughed at. "Church boys," they called us. In addition, I loved to play sports, specifically basketball because I was good at it.

Although we were good boys being raised in the church, my grandmother denied us the opportunity to participate in any outside activities. My brother and I didn't have the chance to participate in AAU basketball leagues, piano, singing, or several of the hobbies we quickly came to admire. It wasn't until I got older that I understood why she shielded me from various opportunities. I may not agree with every decision she made, but I do know that she did everything in her power to protect me from dangers seen and unseen. As you can see there is a pattern developing of us being denied the opportunity to develop in skills that could have provided growth and direction as a young man.

My grandmother was stricter on us because my mother got pregnant with me at the age of 17 and had my brother Derek shortly after. Several of her radical rules were simply to ensure that we didn't go down the same path. If we weren't in school, we were in church.

Moving into my teen years, I began developing a low-self-esteem. I was teased a lot in my childhood, and felt that my dark skin contributed to my "unattractiveness." Unattractive because that is what I was told that by my peers on a consistent basis. My brother Derek was light skinned so he got a lot of positive attention from family members and peers.

> *The reason rejection hurts so much is because we never see it coming.*

I recall my great grandmother saying I would never get married. This was a person that I loved and respected figuratively speaking death over me. Thankfully, I had a cousin that served as a mentor and big brother. He would look out for me and genuinely displayed his care for me. I admired his style and how he carried himself. I don't blame my great grandmother for her comment, because it was how she was raised. She was from the south and dark skinned blacks were treated differently from light skinned blacks.

He was dating a young lady who had a sister in need of a prom date. With my brother and I being similar in age to her, we were the potential candidates. I expected my cousin to ask me out of favor, but was overlooked and witnessed by cousin asking my brother to take her. This was a case of me, once again, feeling rejected by someone I loved and respected. Do you see a pattern here? There were several people that looked out for me and my brother. There were father figures in our life. But on several occasions the men that I loved and respected didn't see enough in me to date female members of their family. This contributed significantly to my self-esteem.

When it was time for me to graduate from high school, the plan was to attend Indiana State University. When my grandmother developed Alzheimer's my junior year this greatly altered my post-graduation plans. The night of my senior year graduation, I received my high school diploma then became homeless the next day. My aunt, my grandmother's daughter, came and took her to Chicago to live with her. I watched all my friends go to college, while I had to stay home in Indianapolis to find a job and place to stay.

Soon after I began hanging with the wrong crowds (low self-esteem) and transitioned from a young man who vowed to never touch alcohol or drugs to being fully addicted to drugs. My addiction took over 20 years of my life. I left the church and was just out in the world. In 2008 the unexplainable happened and my life changed forever. It was during a thanksgiving service at my church. I was giving an opportunity to give a testimony. And while I was talking the Holy Spirit took control and I began to disclose what I had been struggling with. My pastor got up and said that the Holy Spirit said that I would never struggle with drugs again. God healed me from an active addiction and has given me continued strength to be eight years clean from drugs today.

In 2011 I was counseling clients who may have been in danger of losing their homes due to foreclosure. During that time God began to show me the direction he would take me in. I myself was a newly-wed and recent first home buyer. My wife and I were having struggles early on in our marriage. Most of the clients were also married and appeared to be having issues from due to their financial circumstance. While led by the Holy Spirit, I would share my personal testimony and I would also pray with them, right there in the office. I would start having dreams about teaching and preaching; but it was an outreach environment, not a pulpit. God would give me sermon topics and I could hear myself sharing the Word of God to the people.

This dream happened three times. The third time, the dream was so clear that I jumped up out of my sleep and raised my hands and surrendered to God and said yes to his call. God told me He was giving me unlimited access to people, and when they come to me for whatever reason, that my assignment is to minister to them as led by the Spirit, and that I would be their pastor during our interacting. This call was given under one condition, that I had to live a holy life. A life of holiness is now what I strive for each day. I am blessed to have been ordained for five years now and serve as an elder at Life Restoration Church.

Our faith-tested journey!

Our marriage has had its ups and downs. We have been through financial struggles, insecurities, health issues, and more. On September 24, 2015, Terrell had an asthma attack and literally lost his life twice. Once in the ambulance on the way to the hospital, and once in his hospital room. He was placed on an incubator and in a coma for eight days. BUT GOD. This became my time to grow up while having my faith tested. *And without faith it is impossible to please God, because anyone who comes to him must believe that he exists and that he rewards those who earnestly seek him.* Hebrews 11:6.

It felt as though I was in a spiritual boxing arena. I had punched the enemy out by calling on the name of Jesus until he was defeated. By the grace of God, Terrell was healed, awakened and breathing on his own on day eight in the hospital. He was on a spiritual high and it was amazing. Everything he said seemed as though God was speaking through him. He was crying tears of joy with humble gratitude. He had such overwhelming passion and love for Christ like never before.

The enemy tried to use our brokenness to destroy our marriage

One thing we have always had is our love for Christ and each other. If God brought us through as much as we've been attacked with, he'll do the same for you. We believe that marriages would be improved if those in the marriage become fully aware of who they are in Christ. We now understand and comprehend how God sees us and wants to use us as a vessel in our marriage and in the world. He had to bring us to a place where the only way we could live is through and for Him. In marriage, you must put God first, die to your flesh, and seek God in all you do. He will help you through whatever you go through if you just seek Him. Then stand on the

Word! "I will lift up mine eyes unto the hills, from whence cometh my help." Psalm 121:1. A common theme within both stories is rejection. Rejection is very hard to deal with at times. No one likes it. As a couple who has experienced rejection on several accounts growing up, we have discovered that we brought the scars of rejection into our marriage. But, by the grace of God, we are learning, it's only truly rejection if you come in agreement with the rejection. Rejection is simply you rejecting yourself. For rejection to work in your life, you first must accept it.

Kerri experienced her first taste of rejection when her father abandoned her and left her to fight through struggles with racial identify. Rejection also came from her mother in the form of her excessive drinking, as well as past relationships. Terrell felt rejected by his father, peers, church members, and family members. One could easily say that people who we have trusted with our lives hurt us to our core.

The reason rejection hurts so much is because we never see it coming. We are not prepared for it. We tend to walk into relationships and or situations without guarding our hearts, our minds, and even our bodies. We leave ourselves open for someone to hurt us. The Bible declares, "Finally, be strong in the Lord and in his mighty power. Put on the full armor of God so that you can take your stand against the devil's schemes." Ephesians 6:10.

We believe the enemy used rejection as a tool for deterring us from our divine purpose. This spirit of rejection was a generational curse from both sides of our families. *For our struggle is not against flesh and blood, but against the powers of this world and against the spiritual forces of evil in the heavenly realms.* Ephesians 6: 11-12.

If we equip ourselves with the Word of God, we can protect ourselves from the evil one. This will allow for us to see the rejection coming and to not believe the enemies lies. The Bible declares that we are fearfully and wonderfully made. And if God is for us who can be against us?

Kerri and I have been married for over seven years now and through that time God has developed us both into mature men and women of God. Due to not being totally healed before entering the covenant, it is safe to say, that we were very immature. The enemy tried to use our brokenness to destroy our marriage. But because of the grace of God, we can stand before you today declaring our love for one another, for our children, and for a God that never given up on us.

This is one of our favorite scriptures in the Bible. 2 Timothy 1:6-13 *There I remind you to stir up the gift of God which is in you through the laying on of my hands. For God, has not given us a spirit of fear, but of power and of love and sound mind. Therefore, do not be ashamed of the testimony of our Lord, nor of me His prisoner, but share with me in the sufferings for the gospel according to the power of God, who saved us and called us with a holy calling, not according to our works, but according to His own purpose and grace which given to us in Christ Jesus before time began.*

This passage is a daily reminder for us to move forward with faith, love, and confidence in God's ministry called marriage. Because no matter what mistakes we may have made, he still called us before time began. So, we now can walk in confidence knowing that it is not by our works, but by his grace and the purpose and the call he has on our life. God Bless!

Prayer for men:
Dear Lord today, I am praying for the MAN that feels like he has no chance to make up for his mistakes. Let that MAN know that you love him and that you have a plan for his life. Father place REAL MEN around that MAN. MEN that have failed, but by your grace, pulled them back up. Place examples around him so that he can see that there is an opportunity for recovery. Allow him to see that his life does matter. In Jesus Name! #BeMen

Prayer for women:
Heavenly Father in the name Jesus I thank you my husband's wisdom, strength, and leadership in our home. I lift him up to you and I ask you to fill him, deliver, nourish, and counsel him through your Holy Spirit. I thank you that you triumph over Satan's schemes and any scars left on my husband's heart. You are a healer and a restorer of his soul. May your perfect love and mercy touch the brokenness of his heart. Help me to be the help mate and virtuous wife you called me to be. One who consistently brings him honor, respect, and encouragement. Please use me to create a peaceful and loving home. Father show me how to reflect your amazing love for him. I pray all these things in Jesus name.
Amen

Endnotes:
Proverbs 22:6 KJV
Psalms 68:5 KJV
Hebrews 11:6 KJV
Psalm 121:1 KJV

*Sarver's bio continued -

Kerri Sarver was born, raised and resides in Indianapolis, IN and is an only child. Kerri is a real estate agent and loves to assist with first time homebuyers. Her passion is to encourage single mothers to become homeowners. Kerri has earned her bachelor's degree in political science along with many certifications in real estate.

A.M. Davis

As a servant of the most high God for over forty years it is Annie Mae Davis's heart's desire to serve God and his people in whatever capacity He would have her do, during her journey on the earth. Annie Mae Davis was born in Birmingham, Alabama to Millard and Ella Mae Davis. As the sixth of twelve children, she is continuously thankful for their support and friendship. She is the mother of two daughters and their families.

Annie graduated from John S. Shaw High School of Mobile, Alabama and attended Talladega College for three years before attending Texas International Business College where she received a certificate of completion as a medical secretary.

After relocating to Indianapolis, Indiana she attended Indiana International Business College, receiving a certificate of competition as a certified nursing assistant. She continued pursing her education and calling by attending New Wine Skin School of Ministry.

As an ordained minister, Annie attends Freedom Christian Church of Indianapolis, Indiana under the leadership of Pastor Raymond Cousins, and has worked as a medical assistant at Riley Hospital for Children in the Development Pediatric Department for over ten years.

To my family and friend I cannot thank you enough for walking this journey with me. From my heart to yours love always...Annie Mae

CHAPTER THIRTEEN

A Melody of Inspired Poetry To God's Glory

The Journey of God's Love for Man

*I*n the beginning, God created all things, and all things were created in love by Him.

As God looked around at everything He had made with love, He smiled and said that's good!

Thus, the heavens and the earth were completed in all their vast array, in all their splendor and beauty, and God looked again with much love and said, "Very good!"

As God continued to create, He kneeled down to create a man formed from dust.

As God formed and shaped a man, with a woman inside, to later pull him out a bride.

In His image they were created; man in God's image, in the image of God, created He him, male and female, created He them.

Breath of life I breathe into you, with all my love I give to you. Now come forth and subdue to take dominion I do charge you. Multiply over the earth for all generations to see, for all families will start from thee. Mother and Father you will be called as you share my love with all. But this one command I must give to thee, life or death these trees hold for thee. So touch not or eat from this one tree, trust my word and leave it be. For great will be the cost and all will see that disobedience separates me and thee. All eyes will open to good and evil as spiritual death at once begins, but because of my love for you, you win. Separated from me, you will be and oh how I will miss thee.

For I will see you through and redeem you back from the enemy's hand, because my love for you never ends. I will set you a bit lower than the angels above and crown you with glory and honor from above.

So you can develop true fellowship, through relationship because of love, my agape love.

Love formed you, so you can learn to love as I do "unconditionally and without constraint," but it will cost you a price - my son will pay.

Perfectly created you were to be because your journey started from me.

"I am, the almighty, who was and who is and who is to come!" The Father, The Son, and The Holy Ghost are one. The Father's heart will be required, this can only be done through my one and only Son. A door will open through redemption plan as my Son suffers at your hand, to pay justice the cost that sin demands. Payment for sin is death, a physical death all must do. But what my Son did for you, took the sting from death that was meant for you. NOW! The grave no longer has victory over you.

Out of love for you I gave the life of my one and only Son to undo what you had done. In your journey back to me on your heart will be, the blood stained banner of his victory. He gave his life to pay the price that man may have eternal life. So a brand new relationship with me, can start from you, because my grace now allows you too. My Spirit will guide you through till your journey's done and lead you back safely into my awaiting arms. And then you will know never alone you were from me as your journey path lead you back to me. Troubles, trials, and tribulations may have been, like a woman travailing and your weeping may have been longer than a night. But you were never ever out of my sight. Some things must be, but forgotten or forsaken you were never to be. No man, no woman, no people, no race, no nation, no one, no not one, will ever be forgotten of me. I know you and your heart. For in the beginning you were created from love and out of love I called you to be, the image of me.

Under your wings my Lord and my God we take refuge

My love for you stared before your beginning begin, for I AM THE ALPHA AND THE OMEGA, your beginning and your end, your past, your present, and your future, your start and finish, your first and your last, as I saw you through eternity past. You see, you were never so far from me that my love couldn't reach thee. Forsaken nor forgotten never were you to be! No matter your race or your place, you will never be forgotten of me. I am your beginning and your end, so look toward me to see you win.

For the Father's love is longsuffering, patient, and kind, so you can do unto others what I have done for you, for to love one another is expected of you. Love must be sincere and kind, as to love your neighbor as yourself, there's no greater love than that. So now you know, The Father's love is truly divine, as it keeps us through hurt, harm, and danger of all kinds.

For God so loved mankind in this way that He gave his one and only Son that day, that whosoever believes in Him will not perish, but will know the journey of God's love for man ends with eternal life for man. "For God so loved the world that He gave his one and only son that whoever

159

believes in Him shall not perish but have eternal life." Amen!

In His Safety

In his safety! A time of rest I find, a time of rest you find, rest we find in the safety of his arms. Women near and far! Hear me loud and clear! A time of rest He calls us to. To rest under the shadow of the almighty. Under your wings my Lord and my God we take refuge. "He, who dwells in the most secret place of the Most High, shall abide under the shadow of the Almighty. I will say of the Lord, He is my refuge and my fortress; My God, in whom I will trust."

Ladies! A time of rest and restoration He calls us to. LONG TIME! LONG TIME! Have women near and far been the ram-in–the-bush, the intercessor, the scapegoat for abuse.

Abuse to our mind, body, and our soul! Some from infancy to adulthood, and as we grew we learned to hide the seed of shame and pain.

The residue left behind from daddies molesting their little girls, brothers raping their sisters, uncles fondling their nieces, and let's not forget our grandfathers from which it came. From the little girl who birthed her daddy's child, he is now father and grandfather to her child. She can no longer hide the hurt, shame, and pain she feels inside as her innocence diminishes, and depression and suicide sets in.

To the brother who takes from his sister, what is not to be given, be it half or whole reminds us of King David son Amnon, who raped his sister Tamar and left her to endure the shame and pain that rape leaves behind, to feel like no one cares about her demise.

To the uncle who invites the niece to sit on his lap, in his heart, he knows nothing good will come from that. A fondle niece she now becomes, to ensure her hurt, shame, and pain has begun.

To the grandfather, the patriarch of the family tribe, only God knows what you hide inside.

But the legacy of shame and pain you leave behind, your sons and daughters are sure to find.
The Bible tells us "the sins of the father will not go unpunished." Visiting the iniquity of abuse, to the third and fourth generations to act out their father's sins.

Women Near and Far! Hear Me Loud and Clear!

As our childhood shame and pain stays hidden within, we live in its shadow allowing the seed to grow. The poison in its vein leaves us vulnerable and open to be consumed, emptied, and broken. Left to be mother and father to our children. After the mental, emotional, and physical abuse has taken its toll, the scapegoat becomes the-ram-in-the-bush, the intercessor. For the head of the family appears to be cut off and the enemy waits for the body to die. Leaving wives without husbands and children without fathers.

Brokenness, and despair fills the air, as our sons and our daughters' sin impairs.

As the ram-in-the-bush in our secret places, the prayer closet to the heart, at the altar, interceding, praying, fasting, weeping and wailing, on behalf of fathers and sons, mankind as one, marriages, families, friends, churches, cities, state, government and nations. *Do we women pray!*

Satan, you will not have our families this day. Even as we feel the weight of the world set heavy on our shoulders.

As the ram in the bush, WE WOMEN WILL PRAY!
As we cry aloud "God how long?"

He answers, "Not long! For your time of rest is here! *Come unto me all who are heavy with the cares and issues of this world and I will give you rest for my yoke is easy and my burdens are light. Cast your cares on me and I will give you rest."*

Rest from the pain of rape, molestation, neglect, and abuse

Rest from drugs, alcohol, and mental abuse

Rest from low self-esteem and self-abuse

Rest from the pain of verbal, mental, emotional, physical, and social abuse.

Whatever hurt you carry I will give you rest." Allow me into that place inside where all your secret hurts hide, and as I open the hidden places in you, as you allow me to my spirit will free you from hurt, harm, and shame, let no residue remain. "For I will quiet the noisy places in your life," He says. "That your sleep may be sweet and your joy made full."

Come my daughters; my brides, into the Bridal Chamber that your rest in me may be restored, renewed, replenished, regenerated, and rejuvenated that your joy and life in me will be in abundance. You will leave this place of rest in me, knowing that nothing in your life is lacking; missing; or broken. As you rest in the shadow of the Most High, you will know that there is safety and rest in abiding under the shadow of the Almighty God! My peace I give to you-my peace I leave with you-may peace abide in you forever more! Forever more! Forever more!

Safe in my arms!

No Empty Existence!

No empty existence is to be,

The man that walks alone,

The women that stands alone,

The child whose smile is turned up-side down,

For all the world to see and think their existence shouldn't be.

The homeless man that walks along the railroad tracks with hardly any clothes on his back. An empty existence he looks to be, but God's love declares no empty existence is to be.

The woman who prostitutes her body to make ends meet, deep down inside thinks no one cares about her defeat. An empty existence she looks to be, but God's love declares no empty existence is to be.

The child who finds he is raising himself, doesn't know he wasn't supposed to be the enemy's treat, left along for the enemy to defeat. To teach him to bear arms and do harm to his peers on the street. An empty existence he looks to be, but God's love declares no empty existence is to be.

A man's life looks empty and defeated when on the corner he stands, with liquor bottle and drugs in hand. An empty existence he looks to be, but God's love declares no empty existence is to be.

A woman's life looks defeated when her choices leads to a downward spiral of despair, disrespect, neglect, and abuse. A reminder of the wrong choice Eve made in the garden too. An empty existence she looks to be, but God's love declares no empty existence is to be.

A child poured into the earth as if unwanted; wrapped in rags, left on the side of the road, or in the garbage dispose. Whose existence was to cease, by whose hands the angle of death sees. An empty existence this was not to be, because God's love declares no empty existence is to be. To every man, woman, boy, and girl. To every race; red, yellow, black, and white. To every social status in life; rich, poor, and in between. To every tongue, nation and generation under the Son. No empty existence is to be, because God's love declares you free!

Declaration!

"Look, the Lamb of God, who takes away the sins of the world, whose blood stains as it covers man in love!" So let us (Mankind) decree and declare the truth of God's word from beginning to end has set us free from the hand of the enemy! So, I decree and declare that the night the Son of

God was taken to be slain for the man that walks along the railroad tracks, for the woman that lays flat on her back, for the child without a smile, for every person born under the Son, Jesus' shed blood declares your victory won, redeemed and set free for all of eternity.

So I decree and declare that the hair pulled from Jesus' face and the scourging that took place, set man free for eternity, from all sickness, diseases, and infirmities. Be it physical, mental, or emotionally so that no weapon, NO WEAPON! forged or formed against us will ever prosper or prevail.

Brokenness and despair fills the air, as our sons and our daughters' sin impairs

I decree and declare that as they spit in Jesus' face, and shaped a crown of thorns to press down on his face, draped a purple robe to increase his load, a reed for a scepter was placed in his hand as they a jeered him "King over the Jewish land." An unbelievable exchange took place, for on to him our sins were placed. His righteousness, for our sin, is now in place.

So I decree and declare we were "Justified" made just-as-if-we-never-sinned, for the Father and man to become one again and as they marched him down the street half naked yet willing to pay the cost for sin, for the cross He carried belonged to them. And as they nailed him to the cross, not a mumbling word came from his mouth. Then they pierced his side to make sure he had died.

So I decree and declare that as they laid him in the tomb, He descended to take back the keys so the gates of Hell will never prevail.

Triumphantly Jesus ascended to sit with the Father again. Sending back the Holy One, to lead, teach, and guide s in all. Trust, "*For he, himself bore our sins in his own body on the tree, that we, having died to sins, might live for righteousness again."* No empty existence is to be, because Jesus Christ died for you and me to set us free to live for eternity!

Amen! Amen! And Amen!

Color Me Beautiful
For that I am

For God's hands created me, a part of his plan. His plan for man as He formed him from dust, to subdue and have dominion over all He entrusts. So color me beautiful because I am, from God's hand created every nation of man in his plan.

We say red, yellow, black, and white, while God says "every shade of color is precious in my sight."

From the darkest of black and brown to the fairest of red, yellow, and white, we are all esteemed valuable in God's holy sight.

So let's stop this racial fight of who's right, in King's own words "Judged not by the shade of color of one's skin, but what lies deep within. For the content of one's character shows the true heart that lies within." For who you are externally reflects who you are internally.

So we fight each shade of color in words and deeds; red, yellow, black, and white, and let's not forget that brown is in this fight. As we say "White ain't always right," and is black beautiful when black power gives up its strength to diminish within, and red, the pipe you smoked was not always full of peace and hope, and yellow, one ninety-nine is the price we pay for something that last only a day.

Red, yellow, black, and white who's more precious in God's holy sight?

Your skin is too dark, while yours is not, not dark enough but pale I would say. Then color me red, yellow, brown, or white because nothing about this fight is right in God's holy sight.

Now will you agree, some words we say can be full

of venom wouldn't you say?

From the Garden of Eden man was deceived to eat the fruit that God said leave be. So this racial fight is nothing new, so let's look at it from God's point of view. God said not to eat from the tree that will cause you to see but disobedient you had to be. Good and evil were released and spiritual death came to be.

Now separation from God is a punishment you see. All was lost as our eyes came open, from the garden man was expelled, and the first woman two sons a fight begun. One brother kills the other, could it have been because of the color of his skin? Nope, but jealousy took the place of color of skin.

Then I heard much evil was released, as the four horsemen were loosed:

Conquest! War! Famine! And Death! Oh my god how did we get in this mess? But in this mess we will be until our deliverer sets us free and put us back with God you see. For on the cross He had to die not for his sins but for yours and mine. For Christ died for redemption's plan no matter the color of the man. For God so loved the world in this way that He gave his one and only Son that day, so that everyone who believes in Him, eternal life they will win, no matter the color of their skin.

Believers of all race are in the family of God, brothers and sisters together with God. For God created every race of man, no matter the color you claim to be. God created the rainbow of color for man to be.

So color me beautiful for that I am a part of God's rainbow as He planned.

So color you beautiful because you are, created in God's image, in the image of God you are.

So color us beautiful as we are. Created in God's infinite plan with beauty and worth, He created us to be what He called us to be. So now look at me and call me what God calls me.

A chosen generation, I am to be, a royal priesthood, my family will be, a holy nation, we will become, a peculiar people we are, as we represent him near and far.
So God colored us beautiful, because we are children of the Most High Emmanuel by far. So let's give up this racial fight of who's right and see God's plan for each man. For God so loved each man that He gave, a man, a man, and a man, three in one, He gives to us just look in the book He gave to us.
Amen!

Endnotes:
Genesis 1; 1; 26-28:31; 2:1; 7-8;16-17; 21;2:17; 22-23; 4:8 KJV
Psalm8:5; 1 John 5:7; 30:5; 91:1-2 KJV
Revelation 1:8; 22:13; KJV
Romans 6:23 KJV
1 Corinthians 15:16; 5:21 KJV
Matthew 22:39; 11:28-29 KJV
John 3:16; 14:27 KJV
Numbers 14:18 KJV
Isaiah 54:17; 2 ESV
1Peter 2:24 NIV

CONTACT THE AUTHORS

Tracy Pruitt
A Daddy's Love…It's Under the Blood
Tracypruitt23@gmail.com

Crystal Moore
Beauty in Brokenness
crystalmoore6181@gmail.com

Devon Holifield
Destined for Greatness
Livingaboveseelevel@gmail.com

Tisha Sanders
Living a Life Consumed by Fear
tishasand@yahoo.com

LaTasha Floyd-White
What's Behind Her Smile?
Givin2016@gmail.com

Jannifer Denise
Finding Glory
info@goLoveLifeWell.com
www.JanniferDenise.com

Ericka Bond
Hey! I Am Good
destinedtowrite4Him@gmail.com

Stephanie Bowie
Who Am I?
Coachstephb317@gmail.com

Betty Fisher
Pain to Purpose
Queenbeu26@gmail.com www.queenbeu.com

Sabrinna Stennette
Breaking Up With Fear
 G.O.Glory@gmail.com

Nicole Evans
Say Yes to Destiny's Call
winninglifetoday@gmail.com
www.**winninglifetoday**.com

Terrell and Kerri Sarver
Broken, But Restored for His Glory!
Terrellandkerrisarver@gmail.com

A.M. Davis
A Melody of Inspired Poetry to God's Glory
sweetann43@yahoo.com

PRAYER FOR THE AUTHORS

Father, I bring before you each author of this book collaboration. These are your sons and daughters who you've set on life's journey for kingdom purpose. They each have unique stories and have come through challenges that have greatly strengthened them. I thank you for the call on their lives and their willingness to share their stories to reveal to others "A Glimpse of your Glory." You've touched their hearts in a special way and for that I'm extremely grateful. You've assigned angels as divine escorts leading and guiding them along the path of righteousness daily. They've now entered a new chapter of their lives by releasing a portion of their stories to the world. I pray your continued protection over their minds and emotions. Remind them daily of the people who are being blessed by their faithfulness. Thank you for the healing and deliverance that comes as a result of the words written on the pages of this book. I thank you that no harm will come near their dwelling. I speak supernatural increase and elevation. Thank you even now for allowing their gifts to make room for them. Open their eyes to new opportunities and strategies to advance in every area of their lives. I call their families, ministries, and future, blessed. Your hand of favor is upon them. Now cause fresh winds of your Holy Spirit to blow to replenish, refresh, and renew for their next leg of the journey. Thank you for allowing their story to give you glory. In Jesus' name. Amen

PRAYER FOR THE READERS

Father I bring before you each reader of this book collaboration. I thank you for every word written that has pierced the heart and soul of each reader. I thank you for releasing your healing power through the testimonies shared. Thank you for cleansing tears and the joy of laughter. I ask now that you will give each reader 20/20 vision into the spirit real for correct insight and wisdom on how to move forward in seeing your glory in their lives. Guide their thoughts and actions to align with your perfect will for their lives. I speak a release to propel them into their calling, purpose, and destiny as they move forward in you. In Jesus' name.

Amen

"Behold, the LORD our God has shown us His glory and His greatness, and we have heard His voice from the midst of the fire; we have seen today that God speaks with man, yet he lives."
Deuteronomy 5:24

AUTHENTIC
IDENTITY
INSTITUTE

LIST OF SERVICES

<u>COACHING</u>

One on One

Group

<u>KEYNOTE TALKS</u>

Live Out Loud (ROAR)

SIGNificance

The Power of Authenticity

<u>CERTIFICATIONS</u>

5D Coaching Certification

Human Behavior Consultant Certification

SEMINARS
5D Authentically ME™
5D Authentic Men
5D Authentic Identi-Teen
5D Authentically Me & You Couples Course
Authentically Me-Bully Free

ASSESSMENTS
(DISC) Personality Assessment
Spiritual Gift Assessment

JOHN MAXWELL CURRICULUM
Leadership Training
Mastermind Groups
Speaking

AIC BOOK PUBLISHING PARTNERSHIP DIVISION
www.authenticinstitute.com

Other Titles Available from Amazon and Authentic Institute.com

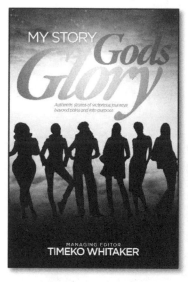

NOTES

NOTES

NOTES

NOTES

NOTES

NOTES

NOTES

NOTES